TEN POUNDS OF GOLD

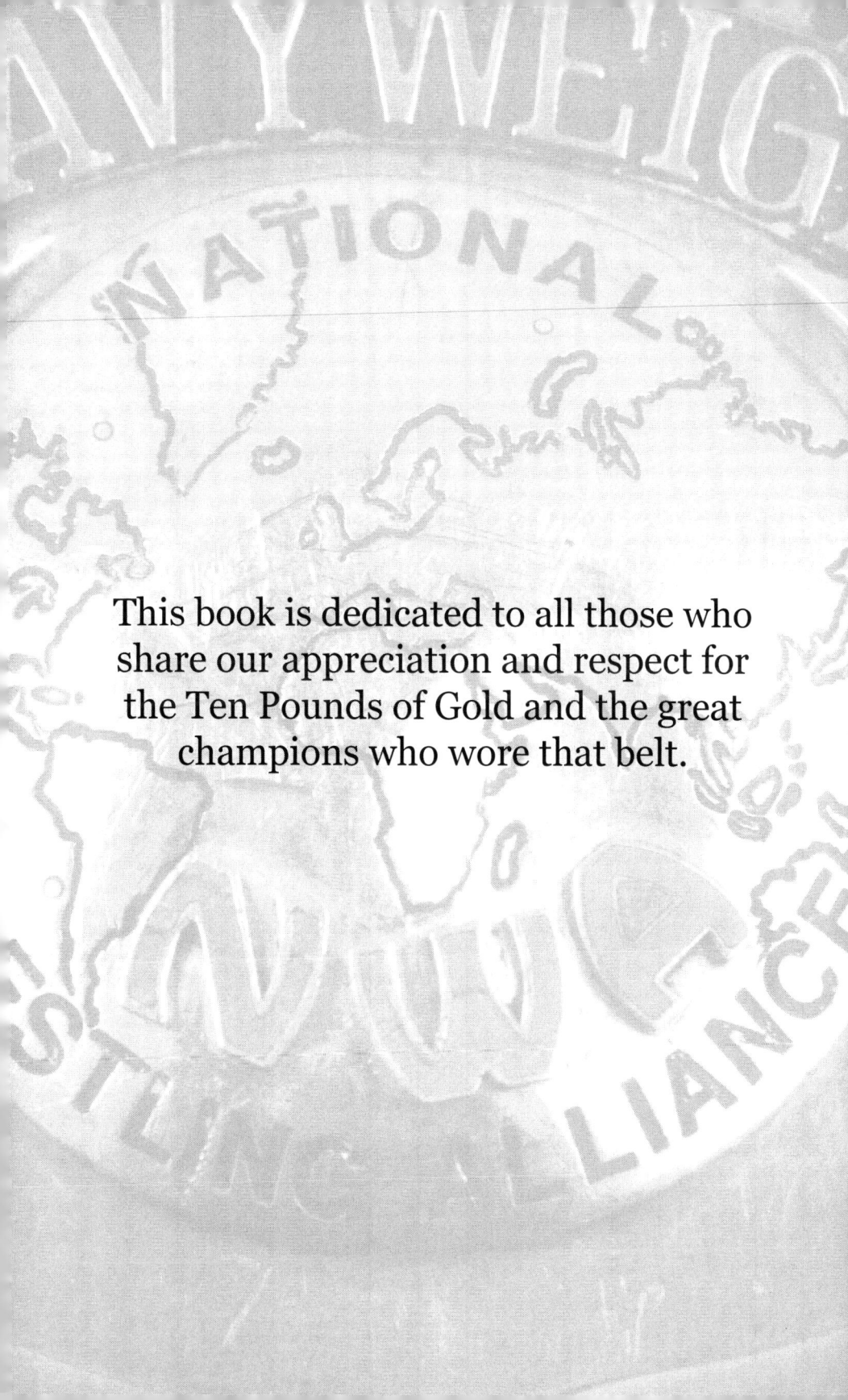

This book is dedicated to all those who share our appreciation and respect for the Ten Pounds of Gold and the great champions who wore that belt.

Ten Pounds of Gold

REVISED & EXPANDED SECOND EDITION

Dick Bourne
with Dave Millican

TEN POUNDS OF GOLD
REVISED & EXPANDED SECOND EDITION
BY DICK BOURNE WITH DAVE MILLICAN
COVER PHOTOGRAPHY BY DICK BOURNE

Copyright © 2009, 2012 by Richmond W. Bourne. All Rights Reserved. Any unauthorized use of material within, including text and or photographs, without specific written consent from the author will constitute an infringement of copyright.

2nd Edition Color ISBN-13: 978-1477521816   ISBN-10: 147752181X
2nd Edition Black & White ISBN-13: 978-1477522813   ISBN-10: 1477522816

Project concept and design by Dick Bourne and independently published by the Mid-Atlantic Gateway. For more information, contact the Mid-Atlantic Gateway at midatlanticgateway@gmail.com. Website address: MidAtlanticGateway.com

For more information on this book and related products, visit TenPoundsOfGold.com.

Editing assistance from Peggy Lathan.
ACCAVER CS.3.2.0.121008

* * * * *

The following works were invaluable resources while doing research for the Second Edition of this book:

"National Wrestling Alliance: The Untold Story of the Monopoly That Strangled Pro Wrestling" by Tim Hornbaker. ECW Press, 2007.

"Brisco: The Life and Times of National Collegiate and World Heavyweight Wrestling Champion Jack Brisco" by Jack Brisco as told to William Murdoch. Published by Culture House Books, 2003.

"King of the Ring: The Harley Race Story" by Harley Race with Gerry Tritz. Sports Publishing LLC, 2004

"Terry Funk: More Than Just Hardcore" by Terry Funk with Scott E. Williams. Sports Publishing LLC, 2005.

* * * * *

Also by the author:
Minnesota Wrecking Crew:
A Brief History of the Anderson Family in Wrestling
Available at MinnesotaWreckingCrew.com

Photography Credits

PRINCIPAL PHOTOGRAPHY

Photographs of the NWA belt taken on October 28, 2008 for this project:

Dick Bourne: front cover, title spread, back cover, 11, 16-17, 59, 61, 62, 63, 64, 106, 107, 138, 141, 142, 143, 144, 145, 146, 148, 150

Dave Millican: 60, 65, 132, 134, 135, 136, 137, 149

Copyright © 2008. All rights reserved.

CONTRIBUTING PHOTOGRAPHERS
(in alphabetical order)

Blake Arledge: Ric Flair robe with NWA belt. (140) Copyright © Highspots.com

Pat Buckley: Ric Flair (99) Copyright © Pat Buckley

Eddie Cheslock: Harley Race (79) Copyright © Eddie Cheslock

Wayne Culler: Ric Flair (back cover, 103, 125) Copyright © Wayne Culler, Slamfest Wrestling Photography

Dr. Mike Lano: Jack Brisco (82), Giant Baba (86), Kerry Von Erich (104), Ric Flair (122). Copyright © Mike Lano at wrealano@aol.com

Rob Riddick: Ric Flair (74) Copyright © Robert Riddick, Jr.

PHOTO AND MATERIAL CONTRIBUTORS
(in alphabetical order)

Terry Funk: Terry Funk (88)

Pete Lederberg: Ruth Oman Collection: Jack Brisco (74), Giant Baba (74), Terry Funk (90), Dusty Rhodes (92). Brian Berkowitz Collection: Harley Race (74) Copyright © Pete Lederberg at plmathfoto@hotmail.com

Scooter Lesley: Harley Race and Gordon Solie (80-81), Jack Brisco and Gordon Solie (back cover, 84), Jack Brisco (85), Terry Funk and Gordon Solie (91), Dusty Rhodes and Gordon Solie (95), Ric Flair (100). Photographs by Gene Gordon. Copyright © Ditch Cat Photography.

Rose Ogle: Program Cover - Tommy Rich (96)

Greg Price: Harley Race and Ric Flair (10) Copyright © NWALegends.com

Harley Race: Provided: Harley Race (back cover, 18, 29, 77), Paul Boesch (21), Sam Muchnick and Boyd Pierce (27, 47), Harley Race vs. Jack Brisco (30-41), Harley Race and Sam Muchnick (51), Harley Race and Boyd Pierce (57).

Thanks also to Harley Race and Mark Eastridge for historical newspaper clippings and to Libnan Ayoub for additional research.

Former NWA World Champions Harley Race and Ric Flair with the Ten Pounds of Gold

The two legendary champions were together for a special question and answer session at the NWA Wrestling Legends Fanfest Weekend in Charlotte NC in August 2009.

The Q&A event celebrated their famous world title match in Greensboro NC at Starrcade '83.

TEN POUNDS OF GOLD
Revised & Expanded Second Edition

Chapter One:	Ten Pounds of Pure Gold	12
Chapter Two:	Houston: Birth of the Belt	19
Chapter Three:	Houston Scrapbook	43
Chapter Four:	The NWA Belt Up Close	58
Chapter Five:	Evolution	66
Chapter Six:	Walking the Aisle	75
Chapter Seven:	Spanning the Globe	109
Chapter Eight:	All The Pieces Matter	133
Chapter Nine:	Reunion	139
Acknowledgments:	At The Gallery	147

Chapter One
Ten Pounds of Pure Gold

It isn't exactly clear when the term "ten pounds of gold" was first used to refer to the NWA world championship belt. Speculation is that broadcaster Gordon Solie may have coined the phrase in reference to the belt early in the title reign of Jack Brisco. Both Harley Race and Ric Flair often referred to the belt that way over their many years of holding the championship. Race carried it one step further: "Ten pounds of *pure* gold," he would say.

Wrestling fans who grew up in the 1970s and 1980s know the phrase well and remember that the "Ten Pounds of Gold" refers to one of the most recognized, iconic symbols in professional wrestling history: the domed-globe version of the NWA World Heavyweight Championship belt.

Today's wrestling fans are also familiar with the likeness of this belt. The modern day NWA adorns its champion with a belt etched in the image of the original. That organization, struggling to regain its footing in an industry dominated by only one major wrestling company, bears no real connection to the territorial

NWA of the 1940s-1980s except in terms of a legal trademark and claims to its title lineage.

THE ORIGIN

This belt's history began in 1973. The version of the belt it replaced had been defended since the late 1950s and was most associated with wrestling icons Lou Thesz, Gene Kiniski, and Dory Funk, Jr. The National Wrestling Alliance decided to have a new title belt made to give the championship a new look. The title was being defended more frequently outside of the United States, and according to Harley Race in an interview for this book, the NWA wanted the belt to better reflect that. Close working relationships established in the early 1970s between NWA members in the United States with promoters in Japan, Australia, and New Zealand resulted in more frequent overseas tours for the NWA champion.

The belt was first presented and defended on July 20, 1973 in Houston TX, when NWA president Sam Muchnick presented world champion Harley Race the new belt before his title defense against Jack Brisco.

Brisco won the title that night, but the road to that special night in Houston was filled with unexpected twists and turns, not only for Brisco, but also for promoter Paul Boesch. These events will be explored further along in this book.

THE CRAFTSMAN

The belt was made by a Mexican jeweler named Manuel Sabala, commissioned by long time Mexican wrestling promoter Salvador Lutteroth. Sabala reportedly also made the 1959 version of the NWA belt. He worked for Lutteroth as a designer and jeweler and even sold tickets for the local matches. Lutteroth was the most powerful man in the wrestling business in Mexico at that time and was a very influential member of the National Wrestling Alliance, hosting a couple of NWA conventions and was always anxious to remain in good favor with Muchnick.

The new belt featured a globe in the center and the flags of the five nations where the title would most frequently be defended: Canada, Mexico, Japan, Australia, and the United States. The dome-shaped globe, however, was the signature feature of the belt, and as a result led to the colloquial description that fans used to describe it - - the "domed globe."

Sabala made many wrestling belts recognized in Mexico. The famous "domed globe" style was his inspiration and is his legacy. Many of the belts in Mexico during that period were in the same "domed globe" style as the Ten Pounds of Gold.

THE CONSTRUCTION

Unlike the way most belts were made then and still made today, the belt was not engraved or etched; it was constructed piece by piece, each part hand crafted by the jeweler. Everything you see on the belt in the photos in this book, from the globe to the flags, from the sections of text to the ornamental swirls, to the sections of beads that outline the perimeter of the main plate were all individually attached to the various plates on the belt.

It was precisely the way that the belt was constructed that helped lead to the relatively rough condition the belt is in today. You will notice in these photographs that several sections of the ornamental beads that outline the main plate of the belt are missing. Through the years, beginning very late in Harley Race's reign as champion, beaded sections were starting to come loose. Some sections appear slightly crooked or out of line. But it wasn't until Flair's reign as champion, sometime during 1982 that some of the sections started coming completely off the belt. By the time Race got it back in 1983, large portions of the beaded perimeter were missing. From the point Kerry Von Erich won the belt in 1984 until the belt was retired in February of 1986, the belt looked almost exactly as it looks today.

RECOGNIZED AROUND THE GLOBE

When first looking closely at the belt, one is struck by how worn and weathered it is. As we prepared to photograph it for this book, we thought about the great venues whose hallowed halls she had graced: from the St. Louis Kiel Auditorium to New York's Madison Square Garden, from the Charlotte Park Center to the Richmond Arena, from Roanoke's Starland Arena to Charleston's County Hall, from the Memphis Mid-South Coliseum to the Meadowlands in the swamps of New Jersey, from the Baltimore Arena to the Dallas Sportatorium, from Chicago's Comiskey Park to Irving's Texas Stadium, from Japan's Budokan Hall to Toronto's Maple Leaf Gardens, from the St. Petersburg Bayfront Arena to the Convention Center in Miami Beach, from the Superdome to the Orange Bowl, and from the Greensboro Coliseum to Kansas City's Memorial Hall. The Summit, the Scope, the Chase, the Omni, and hundreds of high schools, armories, arenas, coliseums, ballparks, and stadiums in between.

It graced living rooms across the country, broadcasting from small studios which hosted loyal, lively crowds sitting on wooden bleachers or in folding steel chairs around small rings - - television studios like WRAL in Raleigh, NC and WTCG in Atlanta, GA.

The fabled champions who carried the belt logged millions of miles on airplanes to countries all over the globe, seven days a week and twice on Sundays. It was arguably the most traveled, respected, and celebrated championship belt in wrestling history during an era where dozens of territories thrived across the United States, and the National Wrestling Alliance saw huge success as its title was defended, as Harley Race would often say, in every corner of God's green earth.

You will also notice in these photographs that the globe on the belt is badly dented. These dents became somewhat of a visual trademark of the belt, and can be seen in most photographs of the various champions with the belt in the last six years or so of the belt's life. There were two different globes over the life of the belt, and both were dented in different places. These dents, and how they were identified in various photographs, helped us define the time line of the different versions of the belt which will be discussed in great detail in a later chapter.

The first edition of this book, primarily sold as a larger hardcover volume, was somewhat intended as a photo journal of sorts, providing as close a look at every detail of the belt as anyone has ever seen except those great champions who wore it.

This second edition serves a broader purpose, not only to present the belt for close inspection, but to also better explore the night it first was presented and defended and the circumstances that led to that point. We also look at promoter Paul Boesch and the special part he played on that night.

Additionally, a new chapter is presented on the title changes

TEN POUNDS OF GOLD

that took place while this version of the belt was in use, spanning the years (and the globe) from 1973 to 1984. We'll look at the grand succession of eight champions through those years, and look behind the scenes at the circumstances that led to each one owning their own unique and special place in NWA history.

"I'm the greatest wrestler on the face of God's green earth."
- *Harley Race*

Harley Race with the version of the NWA world title belt that preceeded the Ten Pounds of Gold. Race would be the last man to step through the ropes and defend this belt.

Chapter Two
Houston, Texas: The Birth of the Belt

CHANGING OF THE GUARD

It was always a prestigious affair when the National Wrestling Alliance would award a member promoter the honor of hosting and promoting a world heavyweight title change at their event. Houston promoter Paul Boesch was given that honor by NWA president Sam Muchnick and the NWA board of directors when it was decided in the summer of 1972 that Jack Brisco would replace Dory Funk, Jr. as NWA world champion.

Brisco and Funk had a red hot rivalry going back to 1966 when Brisco first worked the Amarillo territory for Dory's father, Dory Funk, Sr. The elder Funk had used Brisco to elevate his son, because when Amarillo area fans saw Dory Jr. defeat the former NCAA national champion Brisco at their shows, it cemented Funk's reputation as a legitimate wrestler and contender in the eyes of the fans. Dory Sr. ultimately wanted his son to hold the NWA world title, and a victory over Brisco helped set the early stage for Dory Jr.'s increased credibility as a challenger for the title he would later win from Gene Kiniski in 1969.

The Amarillo experience established the rivalry behind the scenes, but it was their matches in Florida in the late 1960s and early 1970s with Brisco chasing Funk Jr. for the NWA title that set the gold standard for a pro-wrestling rivalry both in the ring and at the gate. Florida promoter Eddie Graham put the two together, and their matches were so successful that other territory promoters brought the two in for title matches in their major towns. Jim Crockett, Sr., was the first to do so, bringing the two in to headline Charlotte and Greensboro, NC. NWA president Sam Muchnick was next to book the two in St. Louis. The results were the same everywhere Funk and Brisco wrestled – box office gold. That fact wasn't lost on NWA member promoters as they debated on their next champion.

Promoter Eddie Graham in Florida became Brisco's mentor and, as a voting member of the board of directors of the National Wrestling Alliance, became his main advocate within the political hierarchy of the NWA. In 1972, he began aggressively pushing Brisco to the NWA board as a candidate to replace Funk Jr. as NWA world champion.

Funk had held the title for a very successful four years and was reportedly exhausted from being on the road and away from his family and was ready to drop the title. Funk's father Dory Sr., also a member of the board of directors of the NWA, did not want his son losing the title to Brisco. But the full board (which also consisted of Sam Muchnick of St. Louis, Nick Gulas of Tennessee, Bob Geigel of Kansas City, Mike LeBell of Los Angeles, and Shohei Baba of Japan) voted Brisco as its next champion, primarily off the strength of his long, strong drawing feud with Funk and his strong amateur wrestling credentials. The decision was made soon thereafter to award the title change to promoter Paul Boesch. The Sam Houston Coliseum in Houston, TX would be the site of the change, and the date was set for March 2, 1973.

PAUL BOESCH
& THE SAM HOUSTON COLISEUM

Wrestling Promoter Paul Boesch was one of the most well liked, admired and respected promoters in the history of pro-wrestling. He was well respected on all fronts - fans, wrestlers, and fellow promoters held him in the highest regard. His building was the Sam Houston Coliseum and his town was Houston, Texas. And make no mistake about it, he was a Houston institution. He had been involved in the wrestling business as far back as 1932 and over his six decades in the wrestling business had literally done it all.

Boesch began promoting in Houston in 1966, taking over for long time promoter Morris Sigel after his death. He had worked as an assistant to Sigel since 1947 after his own wrestling career was cut short by an automobile accident. He was also the television announcer for Sigel and became a local celebrity and commercial spokesperson because of it, most famously on KHTV-39 in the 1970s and 1980s. Boesch kept up his announcing roll and became the face of the promotion after taking it over.

His wrestling office, known as the Gulf Athletic Club, was located during this time at the intersection of San Jacinto and Gray Streets in downtown Houston, as many long time fans will remember from TV promos and newspaper ads for tickets.

The Sam Houston Coliseum was one of wrestling's most famous old venerable arenas. Located at 801 Bagby Street near downtown, the arena opened in 1937 and had an official capacity of 9,200, although Boesch occasionally squeezed a few more than that in for wrestling shows. The Coliseum was home to a multitude of different events including concerts, professional hockey, basketball, boxing, and the circus. But most regularly and successfully over many years, those hallowed halls were home to Friday night Houston Wrestling promoted by Paul Boesch.

ORIGINAL PLANS CHANGE

In advance of the originally planned title change match on March 2, 1973, Boesch booked Brisco into Houston for several

The Sam Houston Coliseum and Music Hall, Houston, Texas

The newspaper ad for the originally scheduled March 2nd title match between Dory Funk, Jr. and Jack Brisco. The match never took place.

dates to lay the foundation for the change, most notably giving Brisco a huge main event win against Houston stalwart Johnny Valentine on February 9, the stipulation being that the winner would receive a shot at the NWA championship on March 2. Brisco upset Valentine and the stage was set for Brisco to take the title from Funk Jr. a month later.

But the match would never take place. Funk, Jr. was in an accident on his Amarillo ranch a few days before the match, rolling his pick-up truck and injuring his shoulder. He would be unable to wrestle in Houston. Brisco always believed that the story of the injury perhaps was fabricated by Dory Sr. so that Dory Jr. wouldn't have to lose the title to him. Brisco was very disappointed at being so close to getting the title, and then having the rug pulled out from under him. Dory Jr. returned to action in early May and Dory Sr. arranged for him to drop the title to another top contender, Harley Race. The match took place on May 24 at Memorial Hall in Race's hometown of Kansas City, KS. The Funks had effectively dodged a rescheduling of the original Houston match with Brisco by steering the title to Race.

The NWA, however, still wanted the title on Brisco and Race would now serve as the NWA's transitional champion to get the title to him. The date of that match was set for July 20, 1973, once again at the Sam Houston Coliseum. Boesch would have a second chance to host and promote a title change.

SECOND CHANCES & THE TEN POUNDS OF GOLD

In the weeks leading up to the July 20 match, Boesch continued to book Brisco into Houston, where Brisco continued to rack up wins against big names like Wahoo McDaniel, the Missouri Mauler, and Blackjack Mulligan. This heightened anticipation of Brisco's upcoming second shot at the title, and the stage was finally set for the showdown with Race.

Not only did Boesch have the responsibility and honor of promoting such an important event in his city, he had the added honor of being the site where the National Wrestling Alliance would present its new $10,000 gold championship belt. The full week before the big card, Boesch had the two local newspapers completely involved in helping promote the contest, and as part of that, highlighted the special occasion of the debut of the new belt. In fact, the presentation of the new belt got as much play in pre-match publicity as the match itself. The newspaper reports attached great significance to this event, as several of the articles leading up to the Friday night card reported that NWA president Sam Muchnick would be traveling from St. Louis to present the new belt to champion Harley Race. Both the Houston Chronicle and Houston Post reported on the presentation of the new belt in their Tuesday editions, four days before the big card.

Although the new belt was first presented this night in Houston and would eventually find its way around the waist of Jack Brisco, it wasn't the first time Brisco had actually had his hands on it. As he describes in his autobiography, he wrestled "Superstar" Billy Graham in Los Angeles about a month before the match in

HOUSTON CHRONICLE

Sports

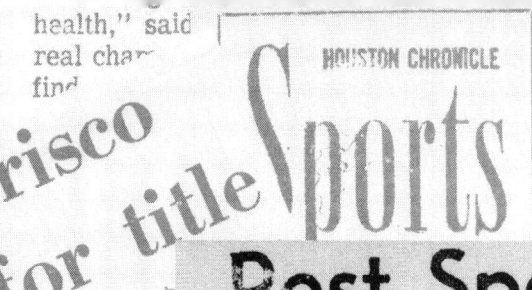

Post Sports

TUESDAY, JULY 17, 1973

Wrestling

Race to get gold belt

With the national spotlight of pro-wrestling focused on Sam Houston Coliseum Friday night, National Wrestling Alliance president Sam Muchnick has decided to use the occasion to come here and present world's champion Harley Race with the new title belt that has been created by a group of artists working in gold.

Race will be given the belt before he faces the country's No. 1 challenger, Jack Brisco and Muchnick has made it plain that from the moment he presents the buckle it will be up for grabs.

"The championship committee considers this to be the most important title match of the year and they decided on my presence here," said the veteran Muchnick who was a newspaperman before he became a wrestling promoter in St. Louis.

Brisco is delighted at the fact that the belt is given to Race before the match.

"He'll be the only champion in history who never had a chance to wear his belt," said the young Oklahoman who is in fine condition for Friday's title effort.

Paul Boesch says that he is in condition for his extra bout with Playboy Gary Hart that will be a special event Friday.

Brisco for title

Race to Risk World Title Against Brisco

Race not worried about Brisco

Brisco wins world

Houston. The construction of the new belt had been completed by Manuel Sabala and delivered from Mexico by Salvador Lutteroth to L.A. promoter Mike LeBell. NWA president Sam Muchnick directed Brisco to pick it up from LeBell and hand deliver it to him in St. Louis. Brisco would see the belt for the second time a month or so later when Muchnick would complete the journey, bringing it with him to Houston to present it to Race.

THE PRESENTATION

There was much fanfare made over the presentation of the new belt that night in Houston. Ring announcer Boyd Pierce introduced NWA president Sam Muchnick to the crowd, and Muchnick made a special presentation of the new gold belt. Harley Race came to the ring wearing the old version of the NWA belt that had been defended since the late 1950s by such great champions as Pat O'Conner, Buddy Rogers, Lou Thesz, Gene Kiniski, and Dory Funk Jr. Now it was Harley Race stepping through the ropes with that historic belt one final time.

In one graceful moment, Race removed the old belt from around his waist and handed it to Muchnick as Muchnick simultaneously handed Race the brand new domed belt that would become known to wrestlers and fans alike as the Ten Pounds of Gold. Race posed briefly for photographs with the new belt around his waist, its glistening gold plates mounted to a strap of leather encased in gorgeous red velvet.

Race's tenure with the new belt would prove to be short-lived. After the presentation of the belt and the ring introductions, Race and Brisco wrestled a classic duel, a two out of three falls contest. Race won the first fall with a vertical suplex. Brisco rebounded, winning the second fall with his famous "unbreakable" figure four leg lock. With falls tied one apiece, Brisco triumphed in the third and deciding fall, hitting Race with the "Thesz press", named for the legendary NWA champion that had been Brisco's idol as a

boy, and who had won the NWA title more times than anyone else in history at that point. Referee Bronko Lubich made the final three count and raised Brisco's hand in triumph.

The Sam Houston Coliseum exploded as the fans realized that they had just witnessed history: the coveted NWA world heavyweight title had changed hands. Sadly, no film or video of the match exists, only the photographs taken that night. Brisco believed Dory Funk, Sr., might have somehow had some hand in that as well, such was the real rivalry between the two camps.

NWA President Sam Muchnick and promoter Paul Boesch both entered the ring. Boesch strapped the new belt around Brisco's waist as ring announcer Boyd Pierce announced the new world champion to the Houston faithful. Boesch himself took several photographs in the ring that night.

Race knelt in the corner, watching the celebration. While he would hold the distinction of being the first to defend the Ten Pounds of Gold, sadly he had the new belt in his possession for only a few brief moments before the match began. Now he watched as the new belt was buckled around Brisco's waist.

That one night in Houston, Harley Race had established his place in history as the first man to wear and defend the new gold belt, and Jack Brisco had become the first man to win it.

*****

On the following pages are photographs taken July 20, 1973, the night Jack Brisco won the NWA title and the Ten Pounds of Gold was first defended.

Race delivers a vertical suplex to Brisco on the way to winning the first fall in their epic 2 out of 3 fall title match.

Race lifts Brisco high in the air before executing a perfect atomic drop.

Jack Brisco backdrops Harley Race.

TEN POUNDS OF GOLD

Brisco staggers backwards after Race delivers a standing head-butt.

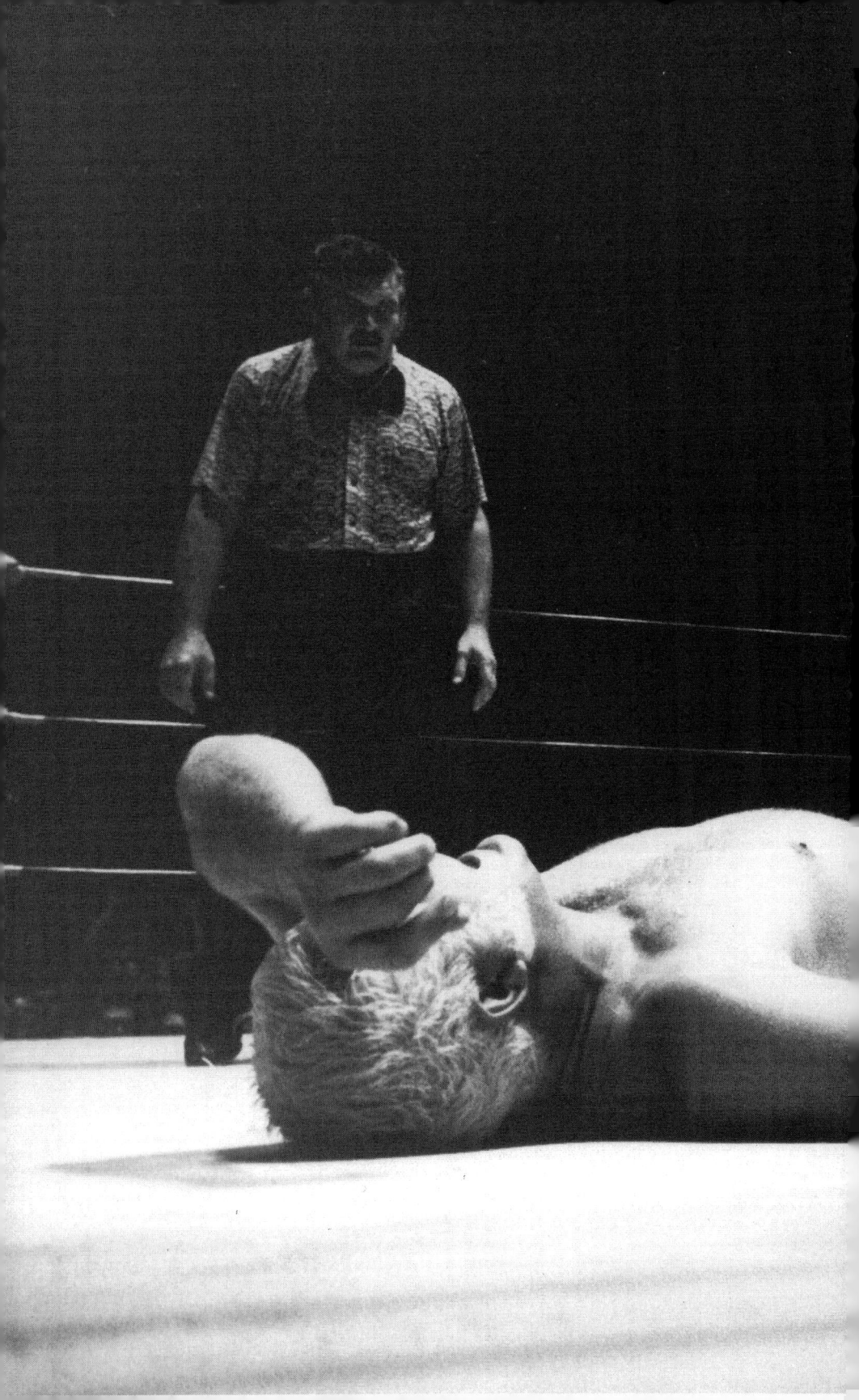

Jack Brisco applies his famous figure-four leg lock to win the second fall.

TEN POUNDS OF GOLD

Race is in rough shape after losing the second fall to Brisco and his figure four leglock.

Harley Race suplexes Jack Brisco.

TEN POUNDS OF GOLD

Race sets Brisco for another atomic drop.

Race goes airborne courtesy of a back body drop from Jack Brisco.

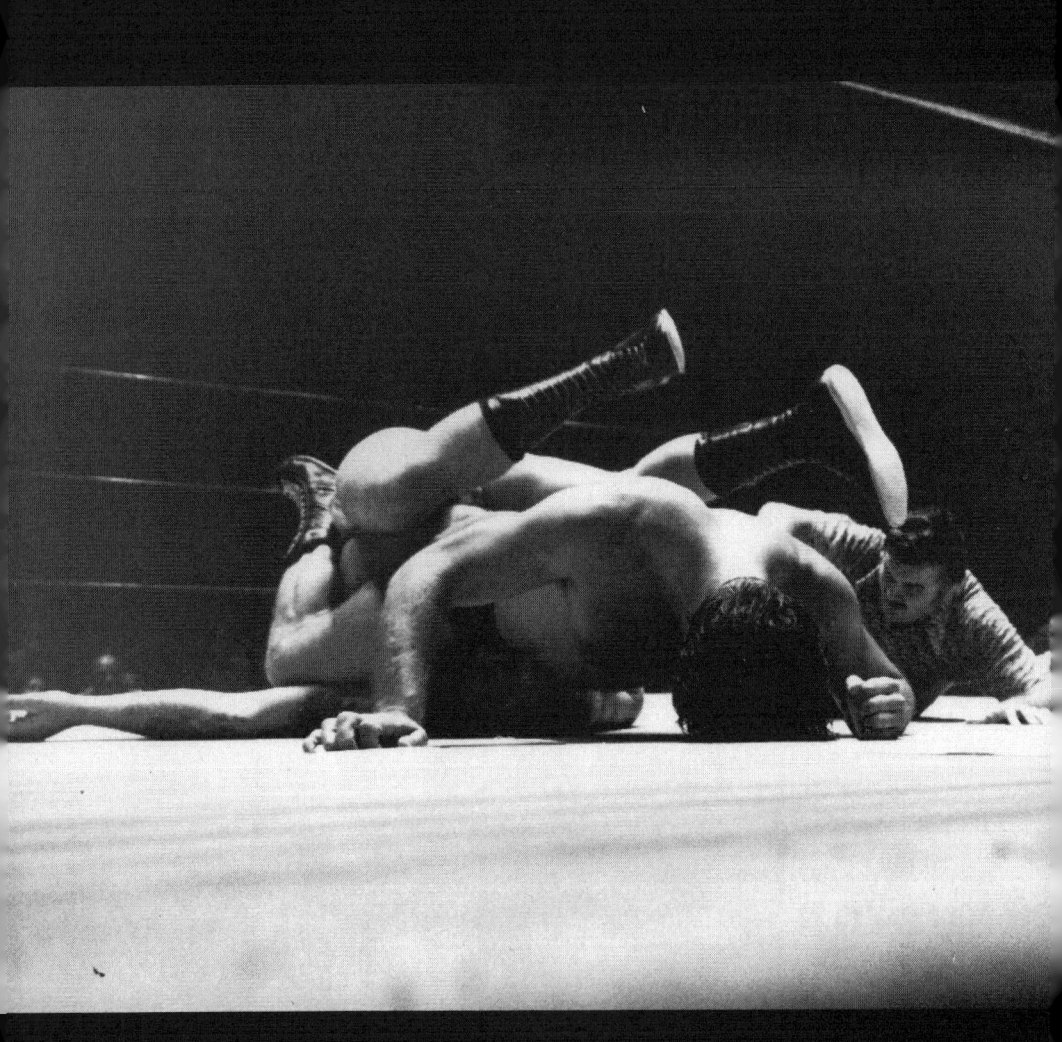

Referee Bronko Lubich makes the three count as Jack Brisco pins Harley Race with a flying body scissors, better known as the "Thesz press", to win the third and deciding fall of the match as well as the NWA world heavyweight championship.

Ring announcer Boyd Pierce congratulates an exhausted Jack Brisco moments after winning the match.

Brisco wins world wrestling title

Race risks world title against Brisco tonight

WRESTLING
COLISEUM Friday — 8:30
YEAR'S MOST SENSATIONAL TITLE BATTLE!
WORLD'S HEAVYWEIGHT CHAMPION
HARLEY RACE
THE MAN WHO BEAT DORY FUNK JR.
MEETS THE NATION'S TOP CHALLENGER!
JACK BRISCO

PAUL "MR TV" BOESCH -vs- "PLAYBOY" GARY HART

NO TV! OF ANY OF FRIDAY'S ACTION

PUTSKI and LOTHARIO -vs- MULLIGAN and MAULER

Chapter Three
Houston Scrapbook

On the following pages are copies of newspaper articles, advertisements, program articles, and photographs related to two nights in Houston in 1973:

> (1) March 2, the night of the originally scheduled title match between Dory Funk, Jr. and Jack Brisco, and

> (2) July 20, the night of the NWA title change between Brisco and Harley Race, and the night NWA President Sam Muchnick first presented the Ten Pounds of Gold.

The clippings for the July 20 card include all of the newspaper reports in the full week leading up to the historic match where the title changed hands and the new NWA world belt was presented.

TEN POUNDS OF GOLD

FRIDAY, FEBRUARY 16, 1973 — HOUSTON, TEXAS

★ JACK BRISCO ★

OKLAHOMA'S SENSATIONAL STAR HAS A TITLE SHOT GUARANTEE BUT CHAMPION DORY FUNK, JR. INSISTS ON NON-TITLE BATTLE!

Jack Brisco proved his right to the tremendous approval he has received from fans, experts and wrestlers around the world when he won over tough Johnny Valentine here last week and earned a contract to face world's heavyweight champion Dory Funk, Jr here next month. It was a rugged battle but a great win for the popular Oklahoma star.

But it did not set well with the champion who did not approve of the manner in which the National Wrestling Alliance granted the title match guarantee to the winner. Dory, Jr. wants a non-title match and Dory, Sr. blames it on promoter Paul Boesch by loudly wailing: "That Boesch is trying to get Junior beat again; he'll never stop trying."

Boesch admits that he has tried to make Funk an ex-champion and will try the same for his successor no matter who it will be. But Brisco already holds a non-title win over Funk and does not want a hollow victory again. "I think I have earned a title chance and the NWA said the man who won last week's match would get one. I want that belt."

Boesch was in close touch with the members of the championship committee of the NWA to get a firm backing to implement their already announced decision, that the Brisco-Valentine winner would get a crack at the title. The long distance wires were humming over the weekend and as this program went to press we were still waiting for the answer.

NATIONAL WRESTLING ALLIANCE INSISTS ON TITLE ON LINE!

Sam Muchnick, president of the National Wrestling Alliance, had a busy weekend with promoter Paul Boesch constantly harrassing him for action on the effort of Dory Funk, Jr. to avoid putting his title on the line against Jack Brisco. Mr. Muchnick, a veteran of many decisions in hot issues like this one, had trouble remaining calm with Dory Funk, Sr. bugging him as much as Boesch! But the official insists that his understanding is that the title must be on the line. He is probing other members and has NWA lawyers looking at the minutes of the meeting and the decision to grant the title test to the winner of last week's bout. "I think the verdict will be in Brisco's favor," he said.

NWA PRESIDENT SAM MUCHNICK

WORLD'S CHAMPION DORY FUNK, JR.

In the weeks leading up to the originally scheduled title match on 3/2/73 between Funk and Brisco, the Houston event programs covered Funk Sr. and Jr.'s reluctance to put the title on the line. NWA Promoter Sam Muchnick was drawn into the fray.

DORY, SR. AND NWA PRESIDENT SAM MUCHNICK WATCH AS THE CHAMPION SIGNS CONTRACT.

Muchnick got Dory Sr. and Jr. to the table for the contract signing, and the title match was set. It never happened due to the alleged injury Funk Jr. sustained on his ranch. This all set events into motion that eventually led to the historic night four months later.

The article at right appeared the night of the scheduled match between Funk Jr. and Brisco.

JACK BRISCO, THE YOUNG CHALLENGER WHO HOPES TO FULFILL A LIFETIME DREAM.

World's Heavyweight Champion On Spot Here Tonight! NWA King Dory Funk, Jr. Faces Sensational Jack Brisco

Dory Funk, Jr. faces one of the toughest jobs he has had since winning the National Wrestling Alliance title when he goes in against sensational Jack Brisco in tonight's main event. Brisco brings youth and experience into the ring with him and erupts into bursts of speed that make him unpredictable and hard to handle. And Funk is well aware of Brisco's potential for becoming the next heavyweight kingpin of the Pro-wrestling world. Jack holds a win over him in a non-title bout and the memory of that loss is one that will haunt Dory, Jr. tonight.

Funk is in top condition for tonight's scrap and we have the pronouncement of his trainers, Dory Senior, a tough taskmaster, and his brother Terry, a chip off the old block when it comes to sound and fury! The earlier effort to turn tonight's tilt into a non-title bout was defeated because the NWA, through its president Sam Muchnick, stood behind their word and would not be swerved by the demands of Father Funk. It was a great demonstration of solidarity by the NWA.

Brisco earned tonight's chance by winning over Johnny Valentine but even without that soundly administered defeat he rates the title try. Brisco is one of the most amazing men in wrestling. He came up through a difficult boyhood to earn his way through college by working on a farm. He whipped heavyweights in high school when he was a sophomore and they were seniors and older and stronger. He was the outstanding wrestler in all Oklahoma in his senior high school year. At Oklahoma State he was again outstanding wrestler of the whole state.

Brisco holds the distinction of never losing as an amateur and holding the NCAA title. As a pro he was first coached by former world's heavyweight champion Leroy McGuirk and former world's heavyweight champion Louis Thesz. And you can include the name of the late Ike Eakins among those who have helped him to this point in his career. But as Jack says: "That is all history, now it rests on this match tonight and I hope to be able to make history with a win."

> **Page 14/D   THE HOUSTON POST**
> *SUNDAY, JULY 15, 1973*
>
> # Race, Brisco battle for title
>
> Harley Race, heavyweight champion of the pro-wrestling world, meets the nation's No. 1 challenger when he faces Oklahoma's Jack Brisco in the final event of a power-packed bill at the Sam Houston Coliseum Friday night.
>
> Brisco, ready to unleash all the frustration of six months of waiting for a promised crack at the title, is primed for an all-out effort. In his climb toward Friday's important tilt he has beaten Johnny Valentine, Wahoo McDaniel, Fritz Von Erich, The Missouri Mauler and turned in a sensational one hour draw with ex-champion Dory Funk.
>
> Race beat Funk for the title in Kansas City and has won over Jose Lothario and Ivan Putski here since that May 24 victory. But Brisco's efforts have not been rewarding until promoter Paul Boesch was able to get the backing of the National Wrestling Alliance to force Race to give Briscoe the title chance he had signed for last March.
>
> Brisco lost his chance to take the belt when Funk had an accident on his ranch.
>
> Boesch will take advantage of the fact that none of Friday's matches will be televised to accept a challenge from Playboy Gary Hart. The special event is added to the regular card.
>
> The Texas state tag team title will be on the block in the semifinal event, a two-three fall fracas, when the champions, Jose Lothario and Ivan Putski battle it out with the tough challengers, Black Jack Mulligan and The Missouri Mauler.
>
> El Gran Goliat, former National champion of Mexico, will return to tangle with Billy Red Lyons; Raul Mata gets a chance to settle things with Blackie Gordman and a c t i o n will get underway when popular George Scott takes on Johnny Fargo in the pace setter.
>
> **HARLEY RACE**

Both Sunday editions of the two Houston newspapers carried advance articles about the upcoming NWA world title defense on 7/20, each giving full details on the circumstances leading up to the big match, and the various challengers both had faced in the prior months.

The Post article featured a photo of champion Harley Race, while the Chronicle presented a photo of the challenger Jack Brisco.

There was no mention of the presentation of the new title belt in the Sunday articles, but that was soon to follow in separate articles days later. The Chronicle announcement is seen above right. The Post announcement is seen back on page 25.

Race to Risk World Title Against Brisco

Oklahoma's Jack Brisco, the nation's No. 1 challenger for the world's pro-wrestling heavyweight title, gets his long awaited crack at the title Friday. He meets champion Harley Race in the final event at the Sam Houston Coliseum.

Briscoe has been campaigning since the first of the year and lost a title opportunity when Dory Funk Jr., who held the title, had to cancel out of a March match due to an injury. Race subsequently beat Funk and took the belt.

The match has been approved by the State of Texas and the National Wrestling Alliance as official and representatives of both organizations will be on hand to certify the decision as official.

Tickets are on sale at 2022 San Jacinto at Gray, 222-2138, starting Monday.

There will be no television of any of Friday's action. Announcer Paul Boesch will take advantage of the night off to accept a challenge from Gary Hart. They meet in an added bout.

The Texas state tag team champions, Jose Lothario and Ivan Putski, risk their belts against the challenge of the Missouri Mauler and Black Jack Mulligan.

Billy (Red) Lyons goes in against El Gran Goliat; Blackie Gordman faces Raul Mata and Johnny Fargo takes on Canada's George Scott to round out the bill.

JACK BRISCO

HOUSTON CHRONICLE Sports
SECTION 3
Sunday,
July 15, 1973

HOUSTON CHRONICLE

Tuesday, July 17, 1973

Race to Receive New Mat Belt

Sam Muchnick, president of the National Wrestling Alliance, will be at Sam Houston Coliseum Friday night when NWA world professional champion Harley Race risks his title against Oklahoma's Jack Brisco.

Muchnick will present a new gold belt that has been made for the NWA championship. He will give it to Race in the ring prior to the match.

NWA President Sam Muchnick (left) presents the new NWA world championship title belt to the fans in Houston Texas.

WRESTLING
COLISEUM Friday—8:30

PRO WRESTLING

TICKETS ON SALE NOW!
2022 SAN JACINTO at GRAY **222-2388**

PRICES IN ADVANCE: $2.00 $3.50 $4.50 $5.50
BUY IN ADVANCE AND SAVE
AT THE DOOR: $2.50 $4.00 $5.00 $6.00

YEAR'S MOST SENSATIONAL TITLE BATTLE!
WORLD'S HEAVYWEIGHT CHAMPION
HARLEY RACE
THE MAN WHO BEAT DORY FUNK JR.
MEETS THE NATION'S TOP CHALLENGER!
JACK BRISCO

| PAUL "MR TV" BOESCH -vs- "PLAYBOY" GARY HART | NO TV! OF ANY OF FRIDAY'S ACTION | PUTSKI and LOTHARIO -vs- MULLIGAN and MAULER |

Post Sports
THURSDAY, JULY 19, 1973

Race not worried about Brisco

World pro wrestling champion Harley Race, expects to make short work of the challenge of Jack Brisco when they tangle in the final event at Sam Houston Coliseum Friday night.

Race is incensed because Brisco has claimed to have goaded Funk into returning to the ring too soon after his injury in an accident.

"Funk was in top shape when I beat him; he never was tougher or in better health," said Race. "I beat a real champion and Brisco will find out that I can beat any challenger too."

Brisco had been waiting for Friday's title shot all year. "I have so much pent up inside of me that is going to explode against Race that I am confident I will win," said the Oklahoman.

A newspaper advertisement and article that appeared in the Thursday edition of the Houston Post, the night before the championship match.

The cover of the wrestling program sold by the Gulf Athletic Club at the Sam Houston Coliseum on the night of the Race/Brisco title match in Houston, Friday July 20, 1973.

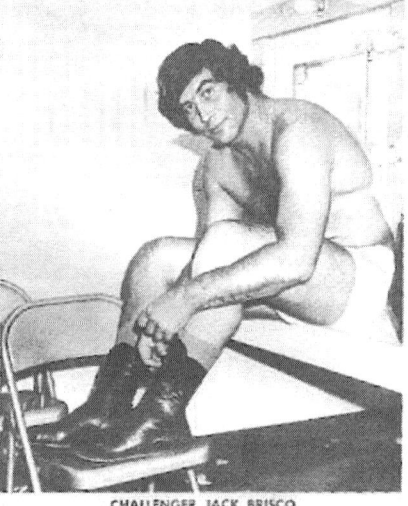

Page 14/F THE HOUSTON POST *Post*
FRIDAY, JULY 20, 1973

Race risks world title against Brisco tonight

Oklahoma's Jack Brisco gets a chance he has sought all year when he meets world champion Harley Race for the National Wrestling Alliance title Friday night in Sam Houston Coliseum.

Sam Muchnick, president of the NWA will be at ringside to award Race a new $10,000 gold belt emblematic of the championship.

Brisco, eager for the match which he believes will make him the new champion, insists that Race will go down in history as the first man to win the belt and not get a chance to wear it.

Race took the title from Dory Funk, Jr., in Kansas City in May. It was a match which the NWA had promised to Brisco. It has been brewing since March, when it was cancelled because of an injury to Funk.

The styles of the two men

JACK BRISCO
promise fans some great championship action.

A special added attraction includes Paul Boesch, who has a night off from his microphone duties since none of the matches will be seen on television. Boesch takes up the often thrown challenge of Playboy Gary Hart. The pair has had a feud simmering for months.

Black Jack Mulligan and his burly partner, the Missouri Mauler, will try to take the Texas tag team title away from the champions, Jose Lothario and Ivan Putski in the two-three fall semifinal.

El Gran Goliat, former national champion of Mexico, returns to face capable Billy "Red" Lyons in the top prelim; Blackie Gordman goes in against a fired up Raul Mata; popular George Scott takes on rugged Johnny Fargo in the first match at 8:30 p.m.

This article in the Houston Post on the day of the world title match briefly touches on every key aspect of the events leading up it. Promoter Paul Boesch did a masterful job in working with the press to promote the event in the local papers.

WE HAVE ONE CENTRAL TICKET OFFICE
2022 SAN JACINTO AT GRAY
WRESTLING HEADQUARTERS

| TICKET SALES WILL START EACH MONDAY OPEN 8:30 - 4:30 MON. - TUES. - WED. - THURS. | ON FRIDAY ONLY OPEN 8:30 - 5:00 AFTER 5:00 AT THE PAVILION BOX OFFICE |

RESERVATIONS INFORMATION 222-2388

CHAMPION HARLEY RACE VS JACK BRISCO

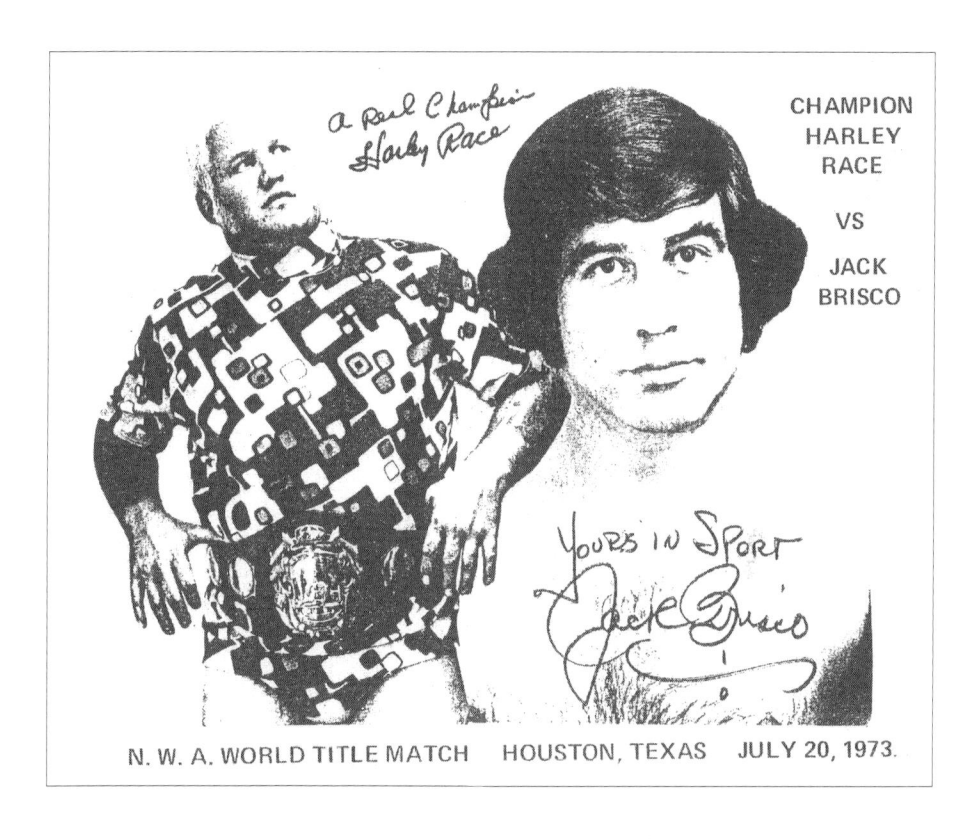

A Real Champion Harley Race

Yours in Sport Jack Brisco

N.W.A. WORLD TITLE MATCH   HOUSTON, TEXAS   JULY 20, 1973.

Race and Muchnick exchange belts before Race's match with Brisco.

TEN POUNDS OF GOLD

YES! THERE WILL BE WRESTLING ON TV! – Ch. 39 –
SAT. NITE — 10:00 - 11:30
SUN. MORN. — 9:30 - 11:00

NWA PRESIDENT SAM MUCHNICK HERE TONIGHT!

Sam Muchnick, who has guided the affairs of the National Wrestling Alliance as its president for many years, is in Houston tonight. Not only is Mr. Muchnick here to see the Brisco-Race bout but his official duty is to present Harley Race with the brand new championship belt which the NWA has had crafted at a cost of more than $10,000. The belt will be given to Race in the ring prior to the title tilt tonight. Sam will also renew many acquaintances here and will be discussing business with promoter Paul Boesch concerning future matches here.

TONIGHT'S CARD
MAIN EVENT
FOR THE WORLD'S HEAVYWEIGHT CHAMPIONSHIP

HARLEY RACE vs. **JACK BRISCO**
CHAMPION — CHALLENGER
254 lbs.—Kansas City, Missouri — 238 lbs.—Tulsa, Oklahoma
2 out of 3 falls — 60 minute time limit

Brisco Gets Title Fight

Harley Race risks his world's pro heavyweight wrestling title when he faces top contender Jack Brisco in the final event at Sam Houston Coliseum tonight.

Brisco has been seeking a title match since the first of the year. He signed a contract to meet then-champion Dory Funk, Jr., but Funk was injured.

Upon recovery, Funk fought Race instead of Brisco and Race took the belt, leaving Brisco still the top challenger without getting a title fight.

National Wrestling Alliance president Sam Muchnick will present Race with a $10,000 gold belt emblematic of the title before the match.

Houston promoter Paul Boesch prepared a blitz of newspaper publicity in both the Houston Chronicle and the Houston Post. Articles began running on the Sunday before the Friday night match, and ran several times during the week preceding the historic card.

HOUSTON CHRONICLE

Page 6, Section 1

Saturday, July 21, 1973

Brisco Wins Mat Crown From Race

Jack Brisco, an Oklahoma-born prowrestling star, entertained the biggest mat crowd of the year by beating Harley Race for the world's heavyweight title Friday night in Sam Houston Coliseum.

Brisco was only one-year old when the title last changed hands in Houston. In 1942 Bobby Managoff defeated Yvon Robert. Prior to that only one previous change was registered in Houston and that was when Bronko Nagurski beat Lou Thesz in 1939.

National Wrestling Alliance president Sam Muchnick had presented Race with a $10,000 gold belt specially crafted for the NWA champion prior to the match. But it was Brisco who walked out of the ring with the trophy.

Brisco came into the pro game with a brilliant amateur record in Oklahoma. He was never defeated in high school or at Oklahoma State where he won the national collegiate title. He went to high school in Blackwell, Okla. where he also was all-state as a fullback.

Race took the first fall but not until he had absorbed punishment from Brisco's repeated arm locks. Race bounced the Oklahomian into the canvas with a body slam to earn the head start.

But Brisco caught Race in his figure-four leg lock, winning the second canto and leaving the champ limping for the start of the decisive third fall.

Jose Lothario and Ivan Putski kept their Texas state tag team title by scoring a three-fall win over The Missouri Mauler and Black Jack Mulligan.

Paul Boesch was declared the victor in his feud with Gary Hart, El Gran Goliat beat Billy (Red) Lyons; Blackie Gordman and Raul Mata drew while George Scott won on a disqualification from Johnny Fargo.

The Chronicle (above) and the Post (right) reported on the title change, as well as the presentation of the new belt. The Japan press (above right) featured full color fold-out posters of the action in Houston.

●NWA世界戦—7月20日（現地時間）テキサス州ヒューストン

JACK BRISCO vs HARLEY RACE

ジャック・ブリスコ（右）対ハーリー・レイス

Page 2/D 　　　THE HOUSTON POST
***　　　　　　SATURDAY, JULY 21, 1973

Brisco wins world title

Oklahoma's Jack Brisco became the first man to win the world's heavyweight wrestling title in a Houston ring since 1942 when he scored a sensational three fall victory over Harley Race in Sam Houston Coliseum Friday night.

The last time the title changed hands here Bobby Managoff beat Canada's Yvon Robert in November of 1942. Before that, Bronko Nagurski defeated Louis Thesz here June, 1939.

Race had won the title from Dory Funk, Jr., in Kansas City on May 24, ending Funk's four-year reign. Before Friday's match, Race was given a new $10,000 gold belt by National Wrestling Alliance president Sam Muchnick, but Brisco's win took the belt from Race before he had a chance to wear it.

Brisco was born in Oklahoma and went to high school in Blackwell, Oklahoma. He was all-state fullback, but also top wrestler in the state and when he went to Oklahoma Sate, he passed up fooball to become National Intercollegiate champion, with an undefeated record.

Brisco led during the majority of the first fall. But the wily Race survived to slam Brisco to the mat and take the opening fall in just over 12 minutes.

Brisco threw everything he had into evening the score. He caught Race in his leg breaker, forcing the man who held the belt to submit.

When they came out for the final fall, Brisco set the pace. When Race threw Brisco into the ropes, expecting to toss him into the air for a back drop, they hit, with B r i s co coming high. The move knocked Race down with Brisco on top and the fall was scored to the new National Wrestling Alliance champion.

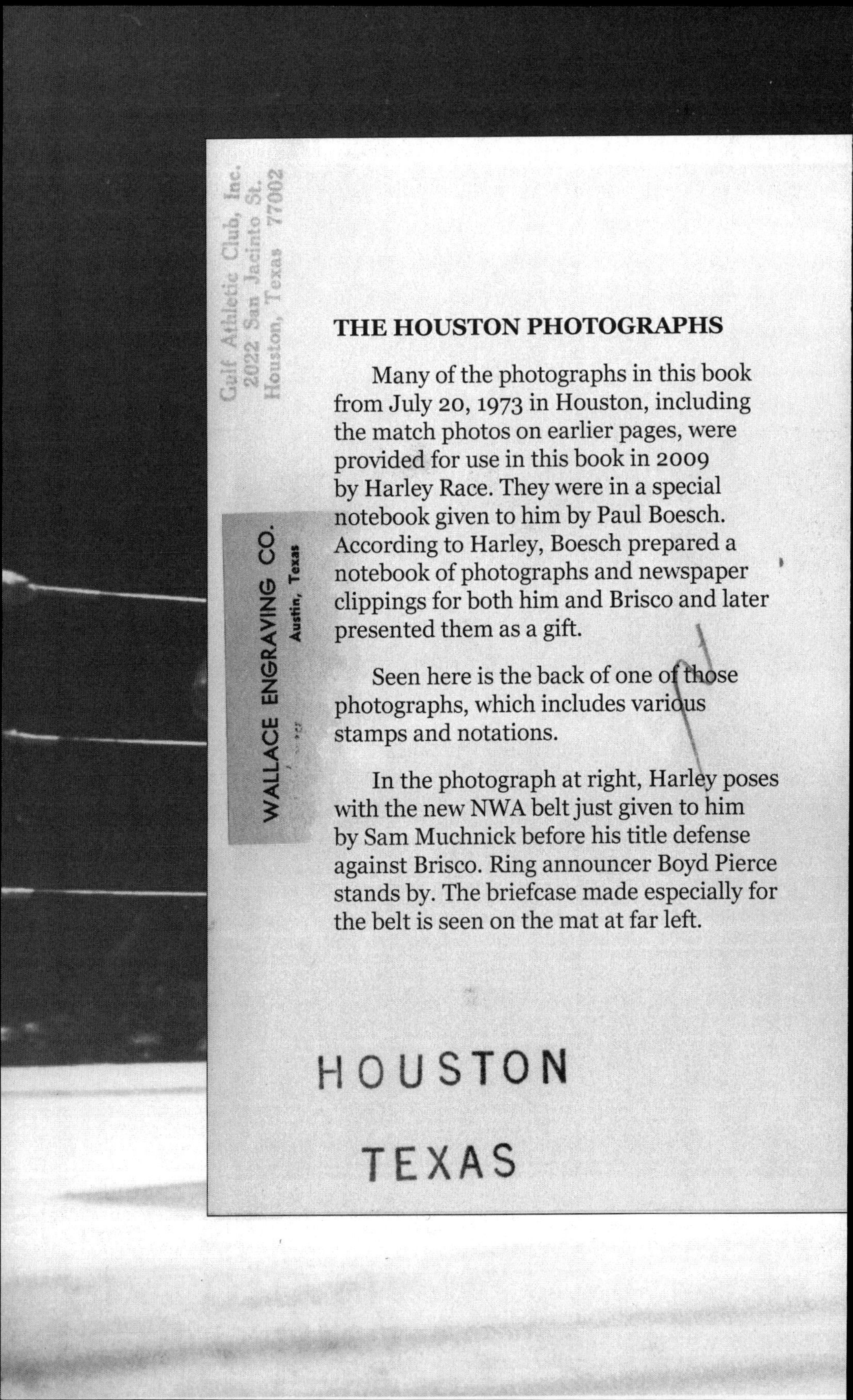

Gulf Athletic Club, Inc.
2022 San Jacinto St.
Houston, Texas 77002

WALLACE ENGRAVING CO.
Austin, Texas

THE HOUSTON PHOTOGRAPHS

Many of the photographs in this book from July 20, 1973 in Houston, including the match photos on earlier pages, were provided for use in this book in 2009 by Harley Race. They were in a special notebook given to him by Paul Boesch. According to Harley, Boesch prepared a notebook of photographs and newspaper clippings for both him and Brisco and later presented them as a gift.

Seen here is the back of one of those photographs, which includes various stamps and notations.

In the photograph at right, Harley poses with the new NWA belt just given to him by Sam Muchnick before his title defense against Brisco. Ring announcer Boyd Pierce stands by. The briefcase made especially for the belt is seen on the mat at far left.

HOUSTON

TEXAS

PHOTO by
PAUL BOESCH
RACE v/s BRISCO
20 July 1973

Chapter Four
The NWA Belt Up Close

The Domed Globe

The NWA belt is distinguished by a domed shaped piece attached to the center of the main plate. This "domed globe" is the feature from which the belt gets that common name.

There were two different globes on the main plate over the life of the belt. The original globe was badly dented in the center sometime during the reign of Jack Brisco. This globe was replaced in late 1976 during Terry Funk's reign as champion. The second globe, slightly larger than the first, was also damaged while in service. It was dented in two spots, one dent much larger than the other. The larger of the two dents is easily seen in photographs of the champions with the belt and is seen in the photographs in this book.

The two globes are easily distinguished from each other by the style of lettering used for the NWA insignia mounted on the globe itself. On the original globe, the letters were level across the bottom of the globe, seen above. On the replacement piece, the NWA letters arched downward, as seen at right.

On the pages that follow are close-up and angled photographs that illustrate how the belt was constructed as well as providing a detailed view of each section of the belt.

HEAVYWEIGHT

NATIONAL WRESTLING ALLIANCE
NWA

WRESTLIN

This photo helps illustrate how each piece is mounted separately to the main plate. Everything you see here - - the ribbon at top that says "Worlds Heavyweight Champion", the onyx panel, the "USA" and American flag peices, the ornamental swirls - - all of these are mounted separately with their own screws to the belt.

The black panel at the top is made of onyx filled inside a gold frame. In the center is a round piece covered in tiny diamond chips. They are set into a silver cap that appears to cover the head of a screw that attaches the black onyx panel to the main center plate.

U.S.A.

CANADA

AUSTRALIA

MEXICO

JAPAN

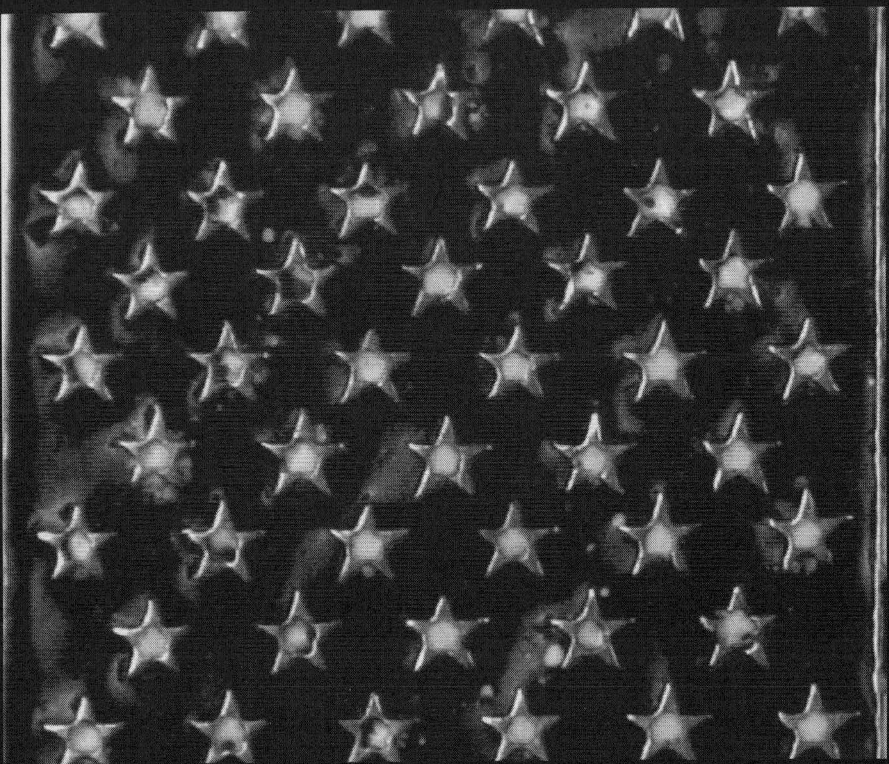

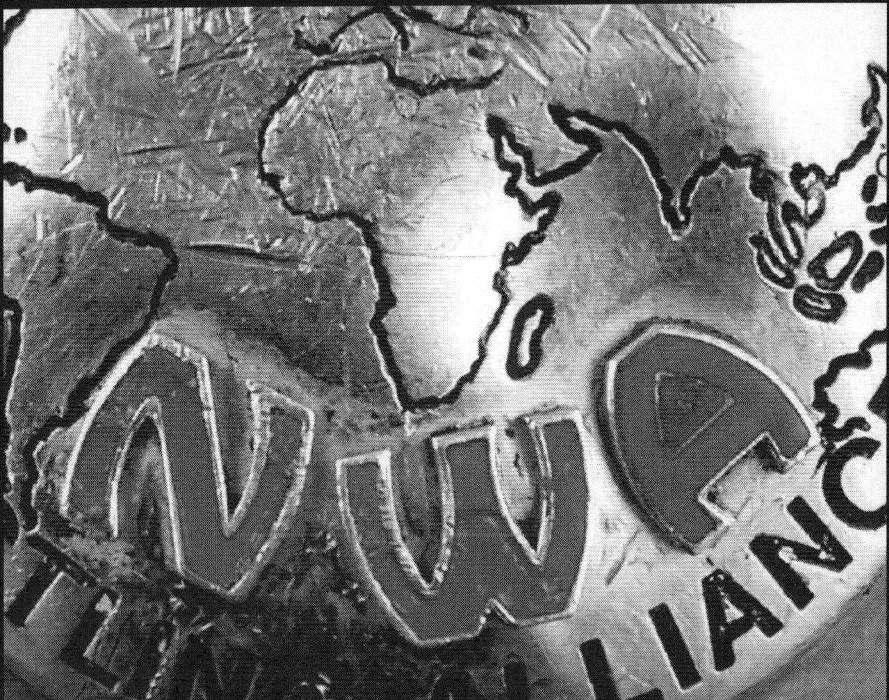

WORLDS HEA...

U.S.A.

Large sections of ornamental gold beads around the perimeter of the belt are missing. In the photo above you can see a single section of beads at the very top of the plate. To either side, where other sections of beads are missing, you can see the holes where screws once attached the sections directly to the main plate.

In the photo below, you can see the entire main plate and the beaded sections at top and bottom clearly missing.

In this image, you see the gap between the domed globe piece and the main plate, indicating further how each piece is attached separately to the main plate. You also get a sense of the thickness of the frame around the black onyx panel. These are the thickest pieces on the plate.

The hex nut that you see at the bottom of the photo is one of two originally used to attach a name plate. Jack Brisco was the only champion to have his name on the belt.

☙❧

Chapter Five
Evolution

The domed globe NWA world championship belt that survives today was not always as you see within these pages. Over the life of the belt, it went through several re-works and repairs, including two changes in leather and a replacement of the outer plates. But throughout its life, the basic design and construction remained the same and each version carried certain elements and characteristics to the next version of the belt so that all versions of the belt are in some way linked to each other.

Unlike more traditional methods of making a belt, as was mentioned earlier, the new NWA belt was actually constructed piece by piece with all the various elements of the design individually attached to base plates. The belt basically had two "layers" of plates. An outer layer was made of gold and that gold layer was mounted to an identically sized layer of steel.

FOUR VERSIONS, ONE BELT

There were four (4) different versions of the globe belt, all physically linked to one another in some way. These will be discussed in detail in this chapter and are illustrated graphically in the chart on pages 70-71.

The four versions are:

> (1) The original red belt in service from July 1973 until likely early 1974. The leather strap was encased in red velvet. The names of the countries were painted with white lettering on a black background.

> (2) Black leather belt in service from 1974 to late 1976. The leather on the first belt was replaced and the red velvet discarded. All of the plates are believed to have remained the same, except for a new name plate.

> (3) Same black leather strap with new or repaired plates (or a combination of both) in service from late 1976 through sometime in 1977. The globe was replaced as well, which included the NWA letters in a different style. The names of the countries were now painted with black lettering on a white background.

> (4) The final version, with new leather, but all plates and the globe remained the same. This final version, which lasted the longest from 1977 to early 1986, is the belt featured in the photographs in this book.

KEY DIFFERENCES IN THE FIRST VERSION OF THE BELT

The first domed globe belt had many characteristics that made it different from the three later versions. One of the most common misconceptions is that the plates were mounted on a red-colored leather strap. The original leather strap was actually encased in bright red velvet fabric (see Brisco photos on pages 82 and 85) which in photographs or at the arenas might have appeared to some as red leather. The two leather straps on the later versions of the belt were no longer encased in fabric and were black leather, but with different colored backing leather.

The original leather strap was cut very wide and did not conform to the shape of the main plate as the later straps would come closer to doing. The cut of the leather did not taper in until well past the main plate, giving this first version of the belt a much wider appearance than later versions.

The main center plate was the same on all versions of the belt with four exceptions.

> (1) The letters that spelled out "N.W.A." on the globe were set straight across on the original globe, and not curved like on the later version of the globe.
>
> (2) The original globe was slightly smaller than the globe that replaced it on a later version of the belt
>
> (3) The areas to either side of the globe were painted black; the final version of the belt would have black onyx panels on both sides of the globe.
>
> (4) The first version of the belt had Jack Brisco's name on a plate attached by two hex-nuts below the word "WRESTLING" on the belt. On the first belt, the name plate said "Jack Brisco" in a combination of upper and lower case letters. On the 2nd version of the belt, the plate would simply say "BRISCO" in all capital letters. For reasons that have never been clear, Jack Brisco would be the only champion to have his name included on the belt. When Terry Funk won the title in late 1975, the Brisco name plate was removed, and sadly there would never be another name plate on the globe design of the NWA world championship.

There were seven grommet-like decorative pieces with solid centers on each side of the main plate on the first belt. These were the only series of grommets on this belt. Subsequent versions of the belt had only three grommets on either side of the main center plate and sets of two grommets between the side plates. These were gold rings with the inside center painted a darker color. Despite the great difference in the placement of these pieces from the first version to later versions, there were the same number of 14 total grommets on each belt.

The side plates with the flags of various countries featured the names of the countries painted in white type on a black background. The same was true for the U.S.A. nameplate over the American flag on the main center plate of the belt. When the plates were repaired or replaced in late 1976 (for the 3rd version of the belt) the plates had the opposite: black lettering on a white background.

The flags of Japan, Mexico, Australia and Canada were in a different order on each version of the belt. (The order of these flags is seen for each belt at the bottom of the chart on pages 70-71.) The flags were separate pieces and it was intended that if a wrestler from one of those countries won the title, their country's flag could be moved to the main plate. The only non-U.S. wrestler to win this belt was Shohei Baba, but in each of his three week-long reigns, the flag was not moved.

The Canadian flag used on the belt was not the National Flag of Canada (a red maple leaf on a white background, with red borders down each side) adopted in 1965. It was the flag of Canada used from 1921-1965, a red background with the Union Jack in the upper left hand corner and a shield containing the coats of arms of the Canadian provinces in the lower right hand corner. It is unknown why the designer of the belt used the old flag since the current maple leaf flag had been in use for almost eight years when the NWA belt was made in 1973.

The original red-velvet belt attached together in back with a traditional buckle. When the belt was re-leathered, they replaced

FOUR VERSIONS OF THE BELT

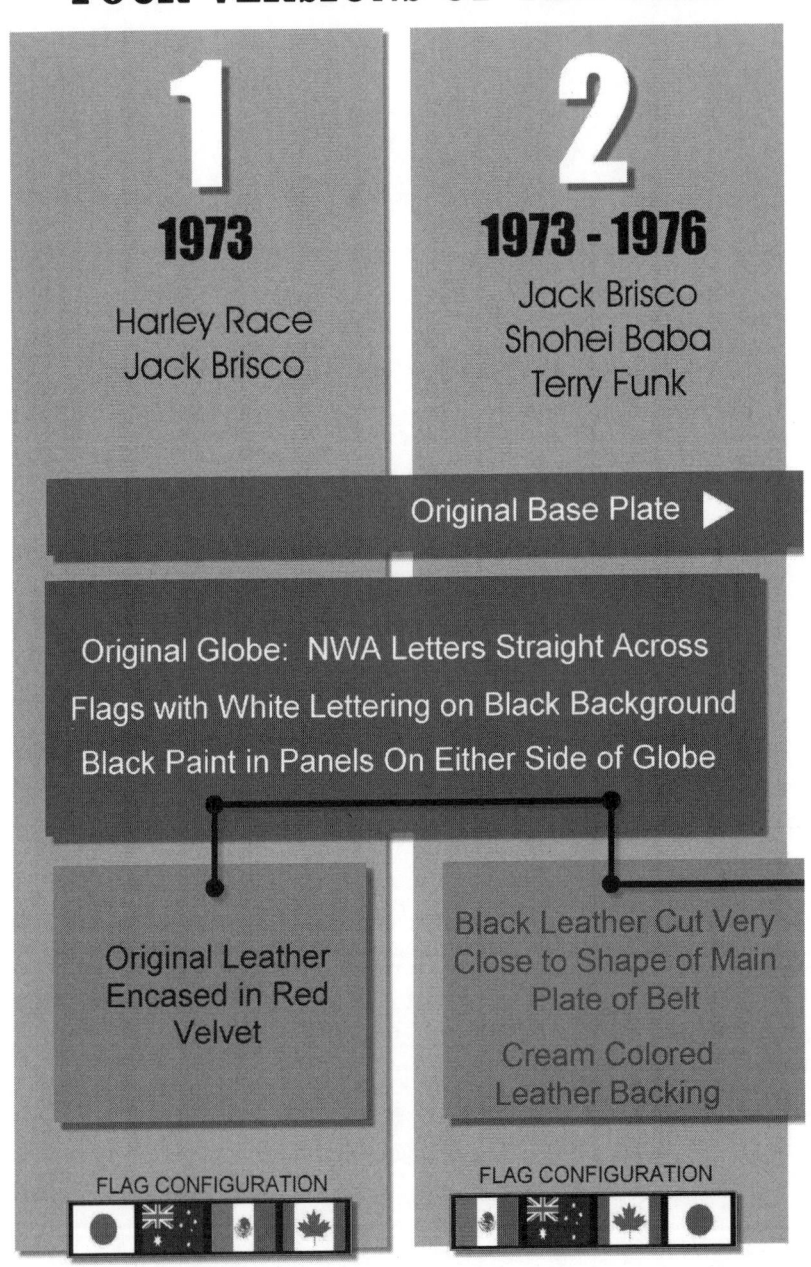

1
1973
Harley Race
Jack Brisco

2
1973 - 1976
Jack Brisco
Shohei Baba
Terry Funk

Original Base Plate ▶

Original Globe: NWA Letters Straight Across
Flags with White Lettering on Black Background
Black Paint in Panels On Either Side of Globe

Original Leather Encased in Red Velvet

Black Leather Cut Very Close to Shape of Main Plate of Belt

Cream Colored Leather Backing

FLAG CONFIGURATION

FLAG CONFIGURATION

EVOLUTIONARY CHART

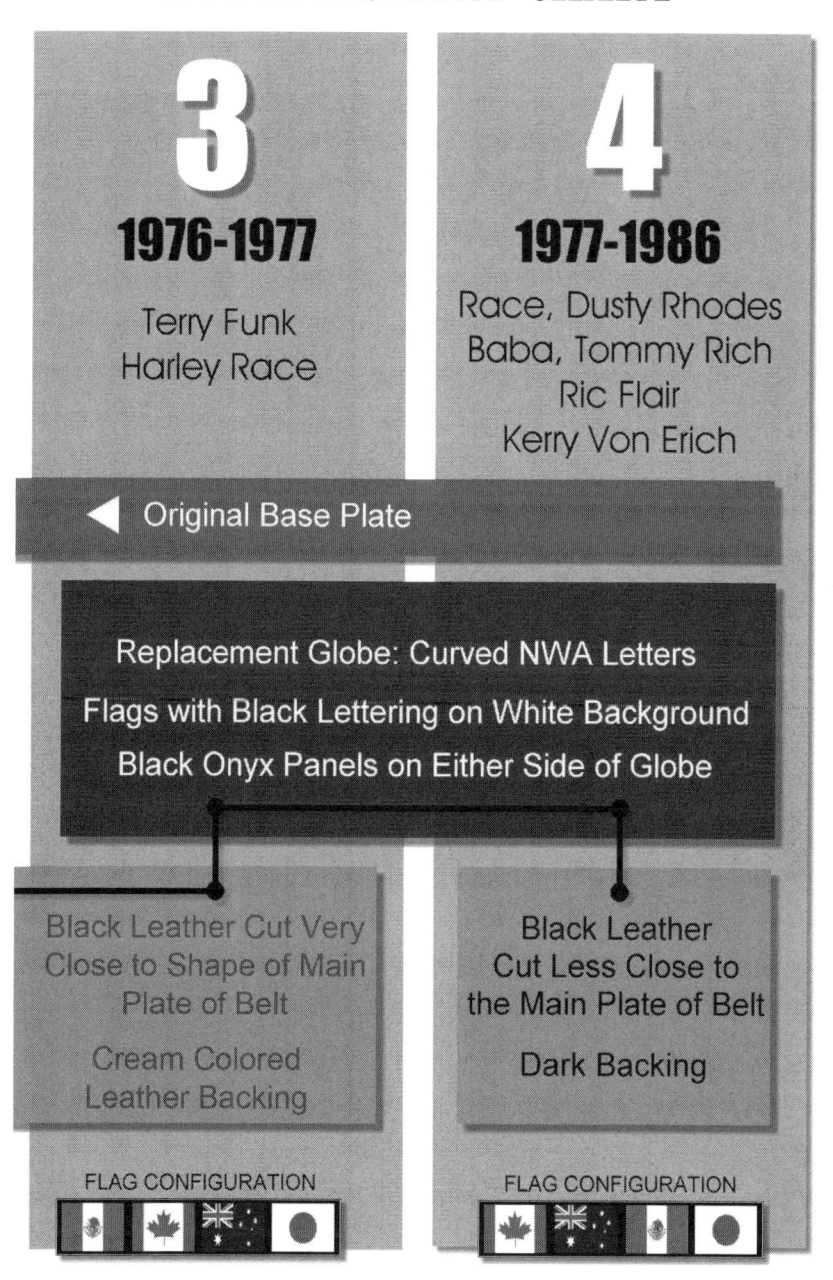

3
1976-1977

Terry Funk
Harley Race

4
1977-1986

Race, Dusty Rhodes
Baba, Tommy Rich
Ric Flair
Kerry Von Erich

◀ Original Base Plate

Replacement Globe: Curved NWA Letters

Flags with Black Lettering on White Background

Black Onyx Panels on Either Side of Globe

Black Leather Cut Very Close to Shape of Main Plate of Belt

Cream Colored Leather Backing

Black Leather Cut Less Close to the Main Plate of Belt

Dark Backing

FLAG CONFIGURATION

FLAG CONFIGURATION

the buckle with a series of five sets of snaps that would attach the belt together in back. When the belt was re-leathered for the third and final time in late 1976, it had an additional set of snaps for a total of six sets.

One final difference: the second version of the belt had cream colored leather backing on the black colored leather belt, which was replaced by a darker leather backing when the belt was last re-leathered.

THE EVOLUTION OF THE BELT

The first major change in the belt was made necessary by the deterioration of the red velvet that encased the original leather strap. A combination of perspiration and general wear and tear, including the packing of the belt into bags with gear damp with sweat, created a moisture problem that led to the rapid breakdown of the red velvet. It was not very long into the life of the belt that the red velvet wrapped leather was replaced with a brand new black leather strap with a much different cut. This second version of the belt also had a new name plate; the one mentioned earlier that simply said "BRISCO" in all capital letters.

During the first year and a half of Jack Brisco's reign, the paint on the belt's plates would slowly deteriorate. The black paint in the panels to either side of the globe was flaking off, as was the black paint backing the white lettering in the country names and various parts of the painted flags. In addition, the globe on the main center plate received a pretty hefty dent right in the center of the globe. This dent, as well as some slight deterioration of the black paint in the side panels, can be clearly seen in photo of Baba with the belt (page 86) when he won the title in December of 1974. By the time Terry Funk won the title a year later, the paint was gone in large sections of the panels on either side of the globe, and the same dent can be seen in the center of the globe (see photo on page 88.)

During Terry Funk's 14 month reign, the black paint in the

panels to either side of the globe all but completely disappeared, and it looked as if the belt might have gold panels to the side of the globe instead of black. At some point toward the end of 1976, before Funk would lose the title to Race in February of 1977, the belt would have much needed work done to the plates, but kept the same leather. In the video of Race defeating Funk in Toronto, you can see the refurbished plates, with a new globe, and the names of the countries over the flags now with black painted type on a white painted background. What is also clear from that video is that the leather remained from the old belt, with the cream colored backing. In the video of Race's win over Terry Funk, the back of the belt is clearly seen, with the cream colored backing worn and even separated from the main leather in places.

These new plates that were repaired or replaced in late 1976 are the same plates that stayed on the belt through the rest of its service until it was retired with Ric Flair as champion in February of 1986. They are the same plates you see in the photographs of the belt taken for this book.

At some point early after Race won the title in 1977, the belt was re-leathered, and that final strap of leather is also the same leather you see in in the photographs taken of the belt for the book. This cut of leather was slightly different than the previous cut. The previous leather was cut very close to the shape of the main plate, as seen in photos of Jack Brisco (page 84) and Terry Funk (page 88) in this book. The replacement leather was cut with a more gradual taper that did not follow as closely the shape of the main plate.

The lacing on this belt was different as well, with a more simple double loop lacing as compared to the more intricate stitching on the previous black leather strap

The chart on the preceding two pages outlines each of the four versions of the belt and illustrates the common links between each version over time.

Race risks world title
against Bri
THE HOUSTON POST
Page 14/F
Brisco Gets
Title Fight
World's Heavyweight
NWA King Dory Fu
BUY IN ADVANCE AND SAVE
TITLE BATTLE!
OTHARIO -vs-
MAULER
CHAMPION HARLEY RACE
Race risks world title
onko Nagurski
beat Lou Thesz in 1939.
National Wrestling Alliance

Chapter Six
Walking The Aisle
The Men Who Wore The Ten Pounds of Gold

Harley Race	76
Jack Brisco	83
Shohei Baba	87
Terry Funk	89
Dusty Rhodes	93
Tommy Rich	97
Ric Flair	98
Kerry Von Erich	105

"HANDSOME" HARLEY RACE

While Jack Brisco was the first man to win the Ten Pounds of Gold in the ring, "Handsome" Harley Race was the first man to actually hold and defend it.

On July 20, 1973, Race wore the traditional belt into the ring in Houston TX for his title defense against Jack Brisco. Waiting for him was NWA president Sam Muchnick who held in his hands the brand new NWA trophy, the Ten Pounds of Gold.

It was a significant moment in the history of the championship. The current belt had been defended since the late 1950s and had been worn by some of the greatest names in the history of professional wrestling including Pat O'Conner, Buddy Rogers, Lou Thesz, Gene Kiniski, Dory Funk Jr. and now Race.

Muchnick presented Race with the brand new belt while simultaneously taking from him the retired one. The new belt stood out with its beautiful gold main plate and its red velvet-

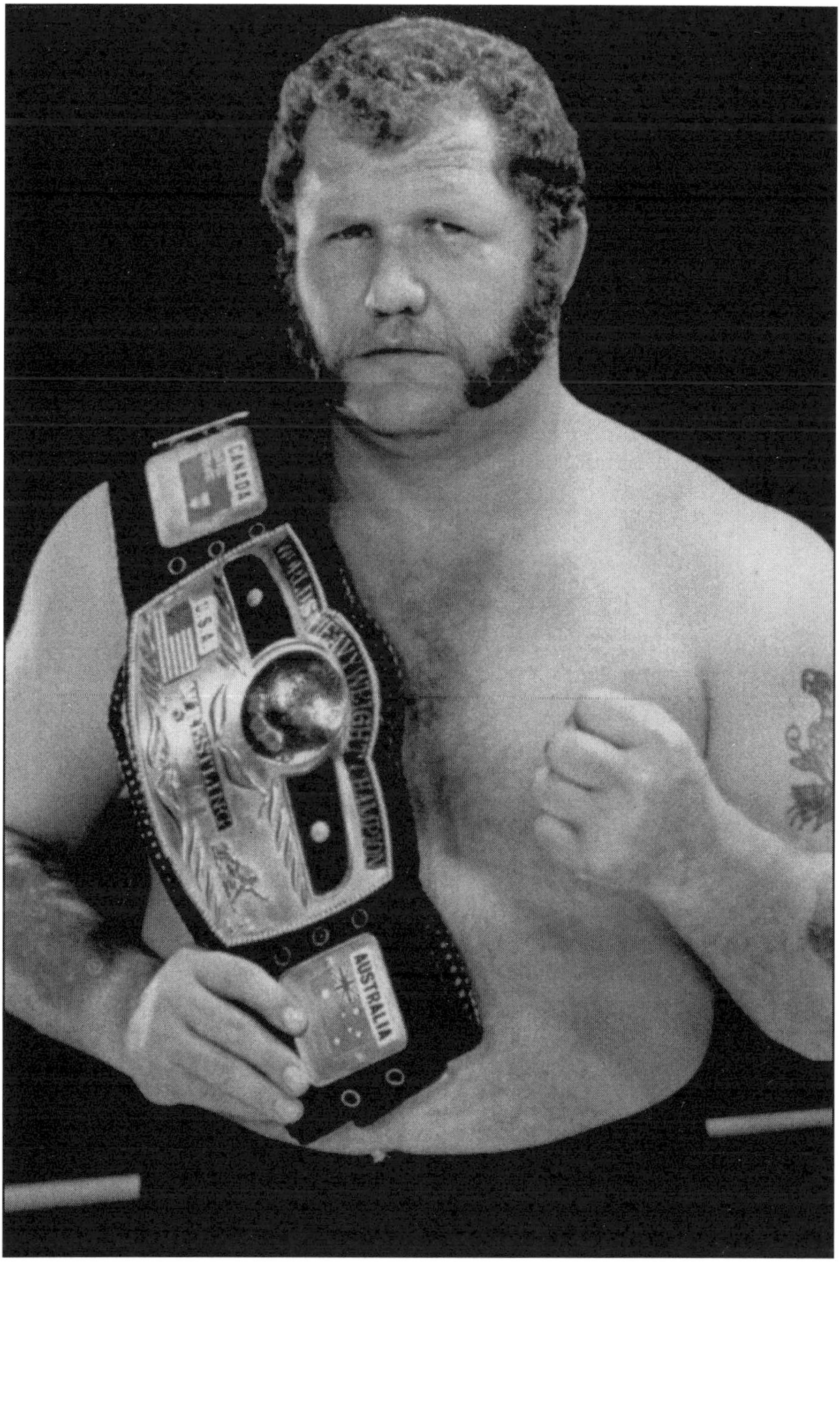
CANADA
U.S.A.
AUSTRALIA

wrapped leather strap. The belt not only represented the United States with the American flag on the center plate, but sported the flags of Japan, Australia, Mexico, and Canada on four side plates.

Race held the new belt in his hands as photographers snapped photos of him beside Muchnick. It would be a short lived moment for Race. He handed the new belt to referee Bronko Lubich and after a hard fought contest, lost the championship that night in Houston to Brisco.

It would be three and half years before Harley Race would hold the belt again. He would strap it around his waist following a victory over Terry Funk in Toronto in February of 1977. That victory began a record setting string of title reigns for the man who perhaps rightfully called himself "the greatest wrestler on the face of God's green earth."

Race was a very successful champion, defending the title for most of the next four years during a time when dozens of wrestling territories were thriving. He became a bonafide legend in Japan, where he is still revered today. He solidified his reputation around the world as one of the toughest competitors to ever set foot in the ring, earning the respect of fellow wrestlers and promoters alike.

Harley Race eventually broke the established record of title reigns held by Lou Thesz, recognized by the NWA then as holding the title seven times. He would eventually be recognized for an eighth title win for a victory over Ric Flair in New Zealand in 1984. It was a very short title reign later recognized by the modern day NWA organization, as well as most wrestling fans, historians, and Flair and Race as well.

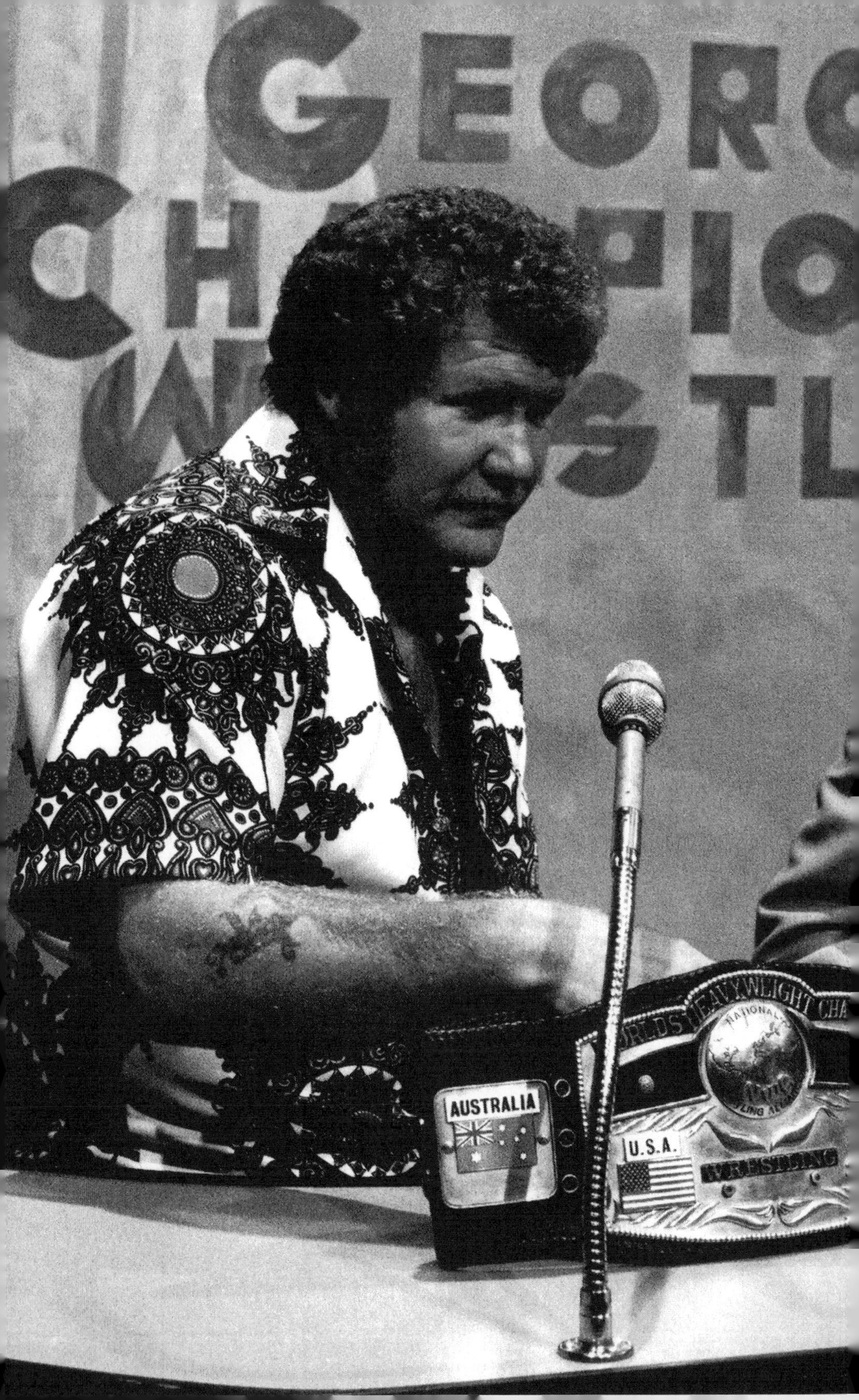
AUSTRALIA
U.S.A.

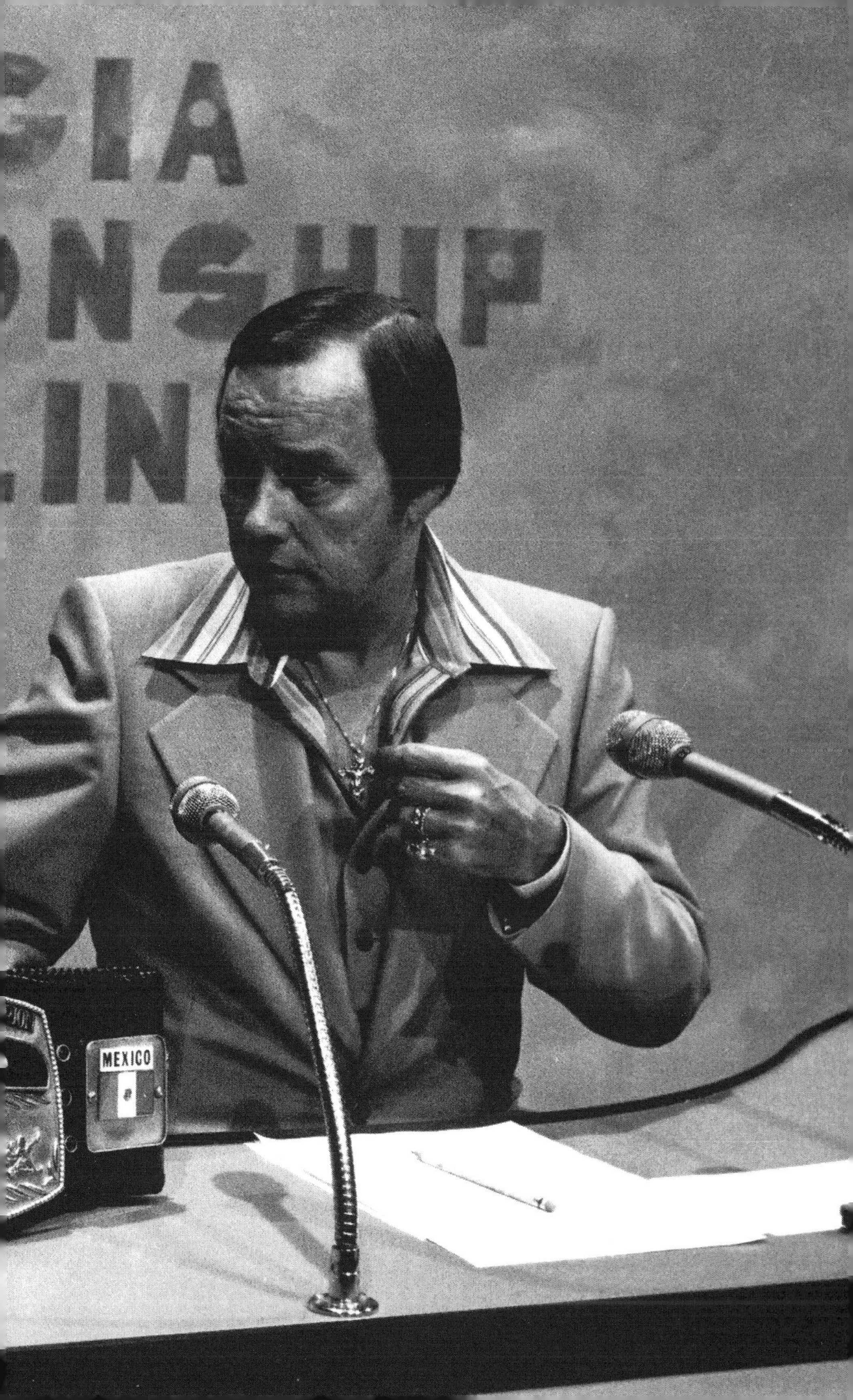
MEXICO

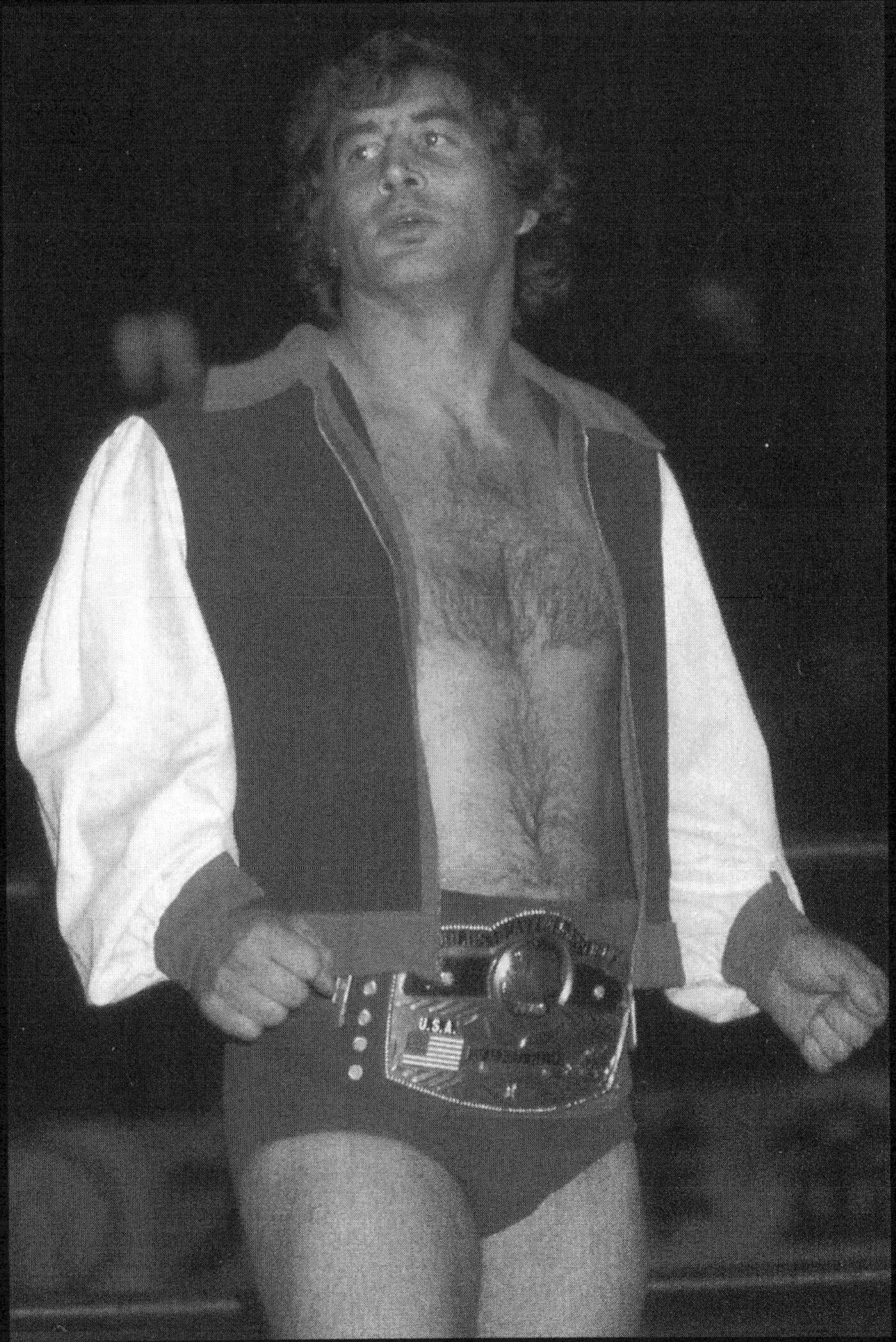
U.S.A.

JACK BRISCO

Jack Brisco is the wrestler most associated with the origin of the Ten Pounds of Gold, having won it in Houston the first night it was defended. (See chapter two beginning on page 19.)

The belt made a big impression from the start, something Brisco related in a story he told in his 2003 autobiography. After a late night flight to Atlanta following his big win in Houston, Brisco was pulled over by the police at 4:30 in the morning only a block from his house. The officer was scanning the inside of Brisco's car when the beam from his flashlight fell on a briefcase on the front seat.

"What's that?" the officer asked. Brisco told him he was a professional wrestler and had just won the world heavyweight championship and the case contained the belt. "The belt was brand new and with all ten pounds of gold shining on that red velvet strap," Brisco wrote. "It was a gorgeous thing in that case. It took away his breath."

"Oh my God, can I touch it?" the officer asked. The new belt had just gotten Brisco out of a ticket.

Brisco's exceptional wrestling ability from a national championship collegiate career gave him instant credibility with fans and promoters around the country and overseas. That meant great credibility for the new belt as well. In Japan, the wrestling press (which was a huge part of the business then) put the new champion and the new belt over like crazy, and Brisco enjoyed tremendous popularity and success there, including many matches with Japan's top star, Shohei "Giant" Baba. Baba briefly won the title from Brisco in late 1974, giving the belt even more credibility both in Japan and the United States.

Brisco made history with his win over Race, becoming the first Native American to win the NWA world championship. Having also won an NCAA wrestling championship, he became the second wrestler, behind Dick Hutton, to win the top championships at both a collegiate and professional level.

He had memorable title defenses against such great names as Wahoo McDaniel, Paul Jones, Johnny Valentine, as well as former champions Harley Race and arch nemesis Dory Funk, Jr., and dozens of others. He eventually dropped the title to Terry Funk in December of 1975.

His two and a half year reign over the sport left its mark and Brisco is still considered today one of the greatest champions ever.

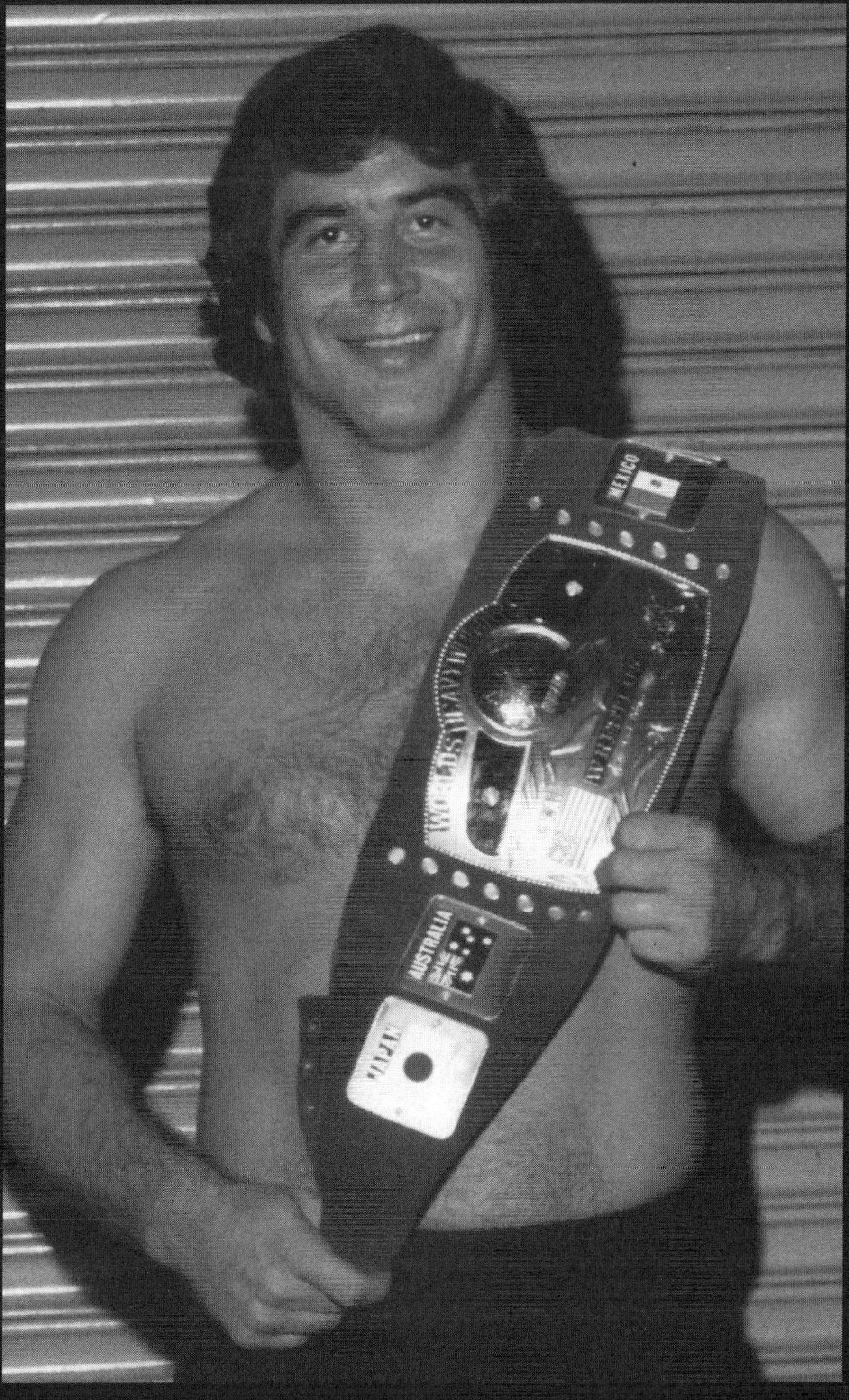
MEXICO
AUSTRALIA

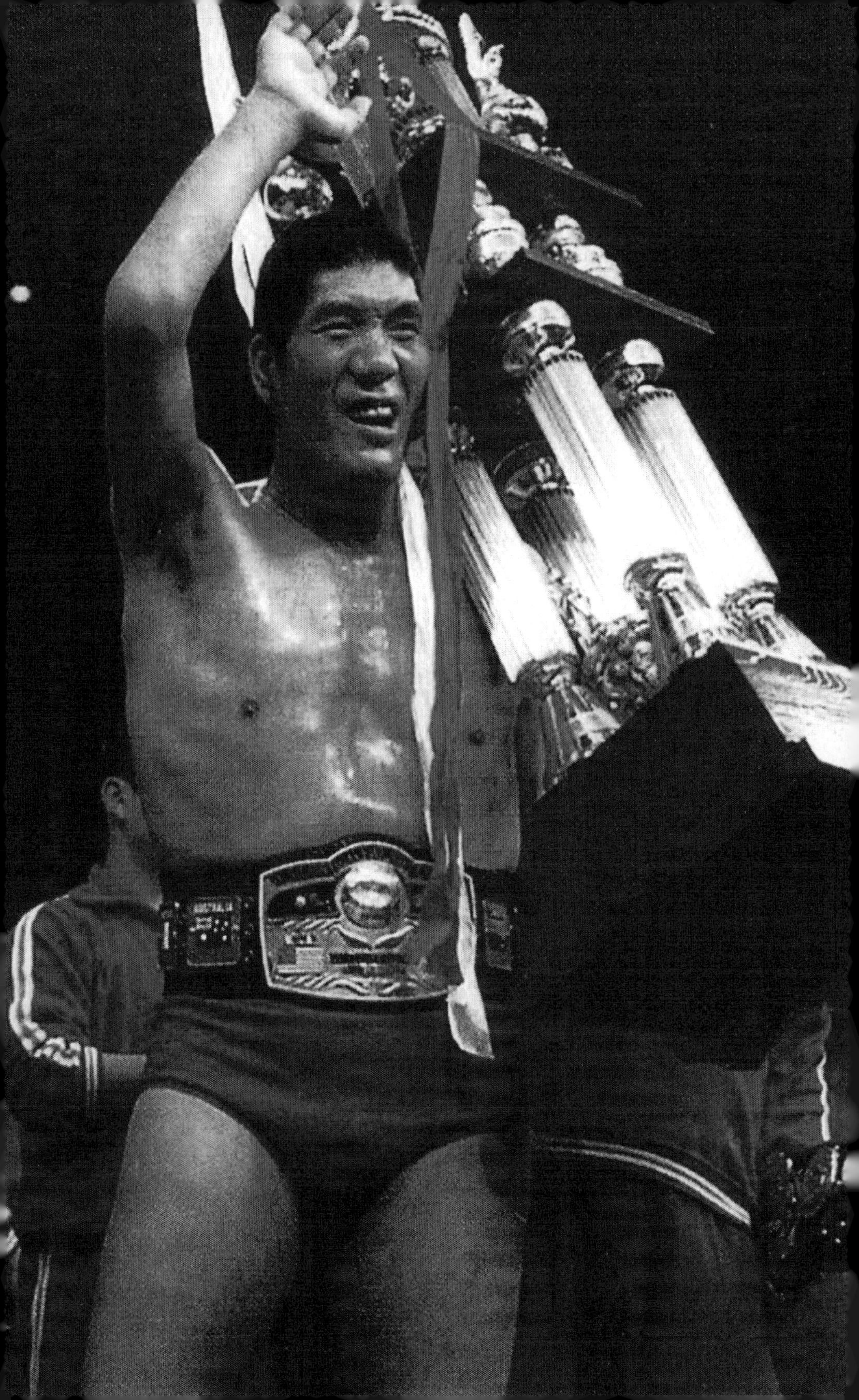

SHOHEI "GIANT" BABA

Shohei Baba was one of Japan's greatest wrestlers and one of the most powerful and influential people in the business. He ran All Japan Pro Wrestling, one of the top two wrestling organizations in the country of Japan at that time. In a strategic move that showed great vision, Baba formed an alliance with several American promoters in the NWA, gained membership in 1973, and presented the NWA world champion exclusively in Japan, where wrestling became a huge mainstream business and was treated much more as a sport than in the United States.

Baba showcased the NWA champions, making bona fide icons out of Jack Brisco, the Funks, Harley Race, and Ric Flair in Japan, all of whom regularly defended the title there and were featured prominently in the country's powerful wrestling media.

He held the NWA championship on three separate occasions, each for five to seven days. Each of those reigns was basically designed to elevate the championship and the title belt in Japan, and to aid him in his bitter promotional battle with rival company New Japan Pro Wrestling. Baba was elevated as well.

His first title win was over Jack Brisco in December of 1974 in a deal brokered by Terry Funk, who helped Baba book U.S. talent into Japan. While most of the NWA board had been apprised of what was to happen by Brisco himself, this was not a title change planned and approved by vote of the board. Brisco and Baba basically went into business for themselves. His second and third reigns were the result of similar arrangements with then champion Harley Race in 1979 and 1980. By that time, largely due to a lack of leadership within the NWA following the retirement of longtime president Sam Muchnick, the practice of the "cup of coffee" title run was becoming more common, and similar situations took place around the same time involving Race with Dusty Rhodes and Tommy Rich. While not condoned by the NWA board, the brief title changes were tacitly tolerated.

Baba's short reigns helped ensconce him as a national legend in Japan and helped him maintain an edge in the promotional wars there.

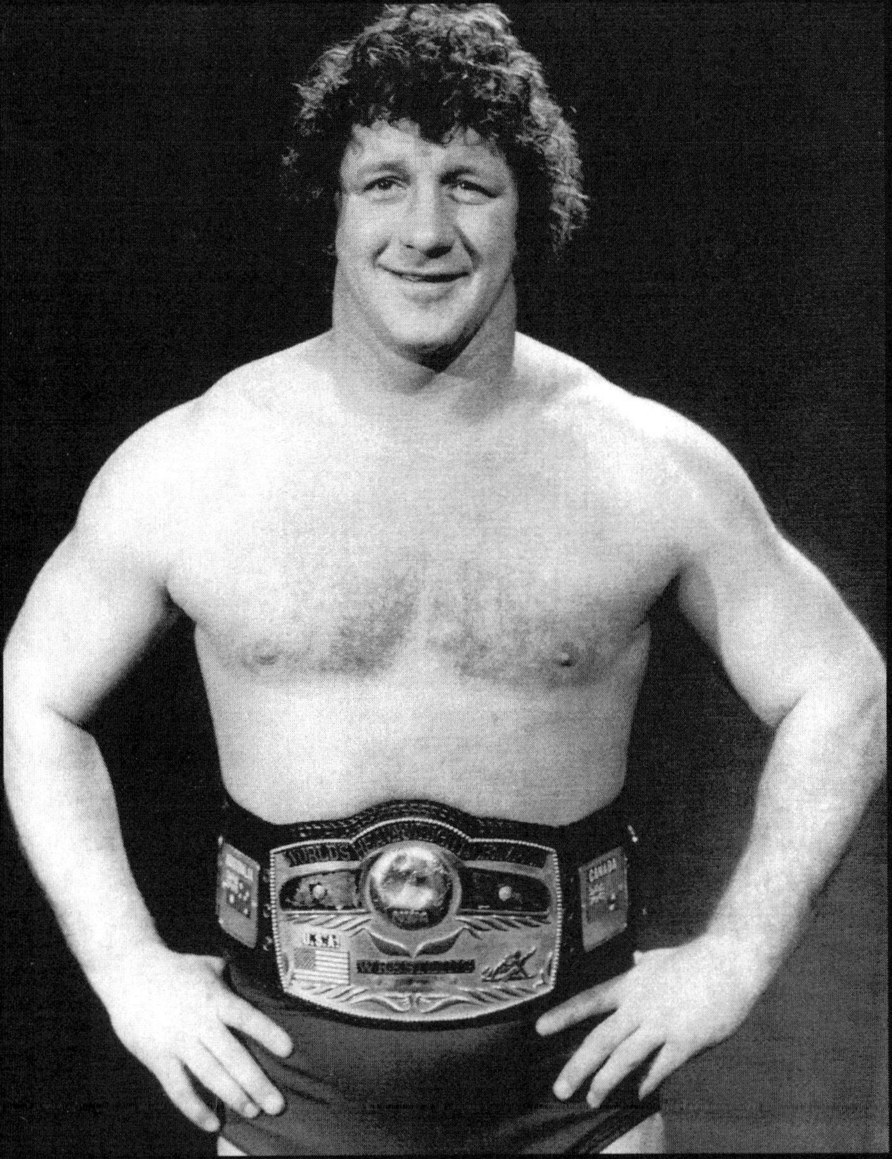

TERRY FUNK

On Wednesday night, December 10, 1975, NWA Champ Jack Brisco was set to defend the title in Miami Beach, FL, against former champion and arch rival Dory Funk, Jr. What fans in Florida didn't know was that Dory was in actuality on the other side of the world in the middle of a three-week tour of Japan. Surprising the capacity crowd at the Miami Beach Convention Center, Dory's younger brother Terry came to the ring and challenged Brisco to meet him instead. It was all part of a master booking strategy for the NWA to replace Jack Brisco as champion, who was exhausted from his two-year non-stop stint with the belt. Terry Funk caught Brisco in an inside cradle as Brisco went to apply the figure four leglock, and became the new NWA world champion. The set-up to the match had served the purpose of protecting Brisco since he could claim he had been preparing all along for a defense against Dory, and it allowed Terry Funk to shock the wrestling world in the process.

History was made that night with Terry's win, as he and Dory Jr. became the only brothers to ever hold the belt in the long storied history of the NWA world heavyweight championship.

With some perspective now over 35 years later, it is interesting to note that Terry's 14 month title reign came relatively early in his career, especially in light of the fact he never held it again. When Race beat Funk in Toronto, many figured it was only a matter of time before the young Funk would regain the title. After all, older brother Dory had held the title for nearly four years. It seemed a near certainty to fans at that time, and probably to a lot of promoters as well, that Terry would get it again.

Not only did he not regain the title over the following 30 years of his career, Funk only seriously challenged for the title once more in what was a memorable series of title matches with then champion Ric Flair in 1989.

TEN POUNDS OF GOLD

December 10, 1975: Terry Funk celebrates following his title victory over Jack Brisco at the Miami Beach Convention Center in Miami, Florida.

90

Above: NWA champion Terry Funk with Gordon Solie.

It would actually be Harley Race, the man who ended Terry's reign, who would go on from there and hold the title seven more times over the next seven years. Race made a bit of history as well with his win over Terry Funk in 1977, becoming the only man to defeat two brothers for the NWA world title.

Funk said later that he had originally hoped to make one big run with the belt, make a lot of money, and retire early from the sport. He has also mentioned that he wanted to get off the road as it related to his family life. He first retired from the sport about three years after losing the title to Race, and has been returning to wrestling and retiring ever since. Funk may never really give it up for good.

Of the eight men who would wear the Ten Pounds of Gold, Terry Funk was the champion who would be remembered as the wildest one of the bunch, blending scientific wrestling with a brawling style that was years ahead of its time.

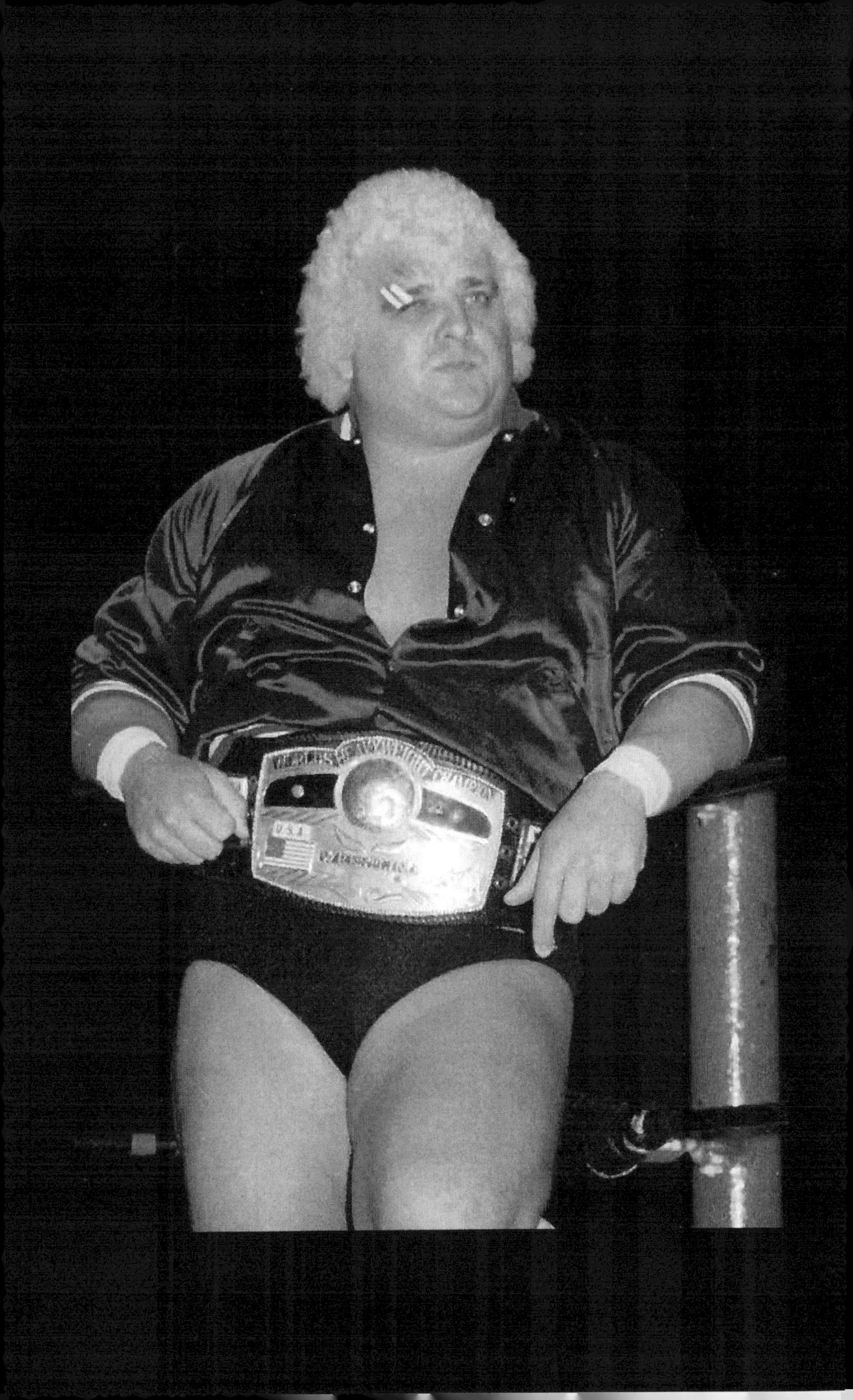

"THE AMERICAN DREAM" DUSTY RHODES

Dusty Rhodes was one of the most charismatic wrestlers to ever hold the NWA world heavyweight championship. He did so on three occasions, although two were very brief and are considered somewhat controversial. Rhodes first title win was part of a series of goodwill gestures by the NWA toward various member promoters during the late 1970s and early 1980s, in this case to Florida promoter and former NWA president Eddie Graham, who was an advocate within the NWA for Rhodes to be made champion. This was in contrast to a wrestler who was selected for championship succession by the NWA board of directors during its annual meeting.

His first title reign was only five days long, winning the title from Harley Race on August 21, 1979 in Tampa FL. Rhodes later regained the title a second time, again from Race, on June 21, 1981 in Atlanta GA. It was this second title reign where Rhodes represented the choice of member promoters. He carried the Ten Pounds of Gold on these two occasions, and briefly held the "Big Gold" version of the NWA title belt when he defeated Ric Flair for a couple of weeks in 1986.

A "bad guy" during his early career, Rhodes became one of the most popular wrestlers in the sport after a turn in the Florida territory. He was one of the top box office attractions in the business during the 1970s and 1980s and promoters all over the country brought him in as a special attraction, similar to the way Andre the Giant was booked. He was one of only a handful of performers who was in that much demand. It was that aura that would seemingly make him a good choice as a touring champion since he was big at the box office almost everywhere he went. But the successful tried and true formula for a world champion at the time was a heel champion entering each territory to face that area's top popular contender, and Dusty's reign was relatively short compared to the many years that champions had held the title in previous decades. He dropped the title after only three months to Ric Flair in September of 1981.

In truth, Rhodes didn't really need the title; he was a big draw with or without it. Wrestling's "every man", the son of a plumber, the "American Dream" was always better in the role of chasing the title.

Dusty Rhodes became one of the most influential people in the business during the late 1970s and 1980s, including creative control in Florida and the Mid-Atlantic, two of the National Wrestling Alliance's most successful territories.

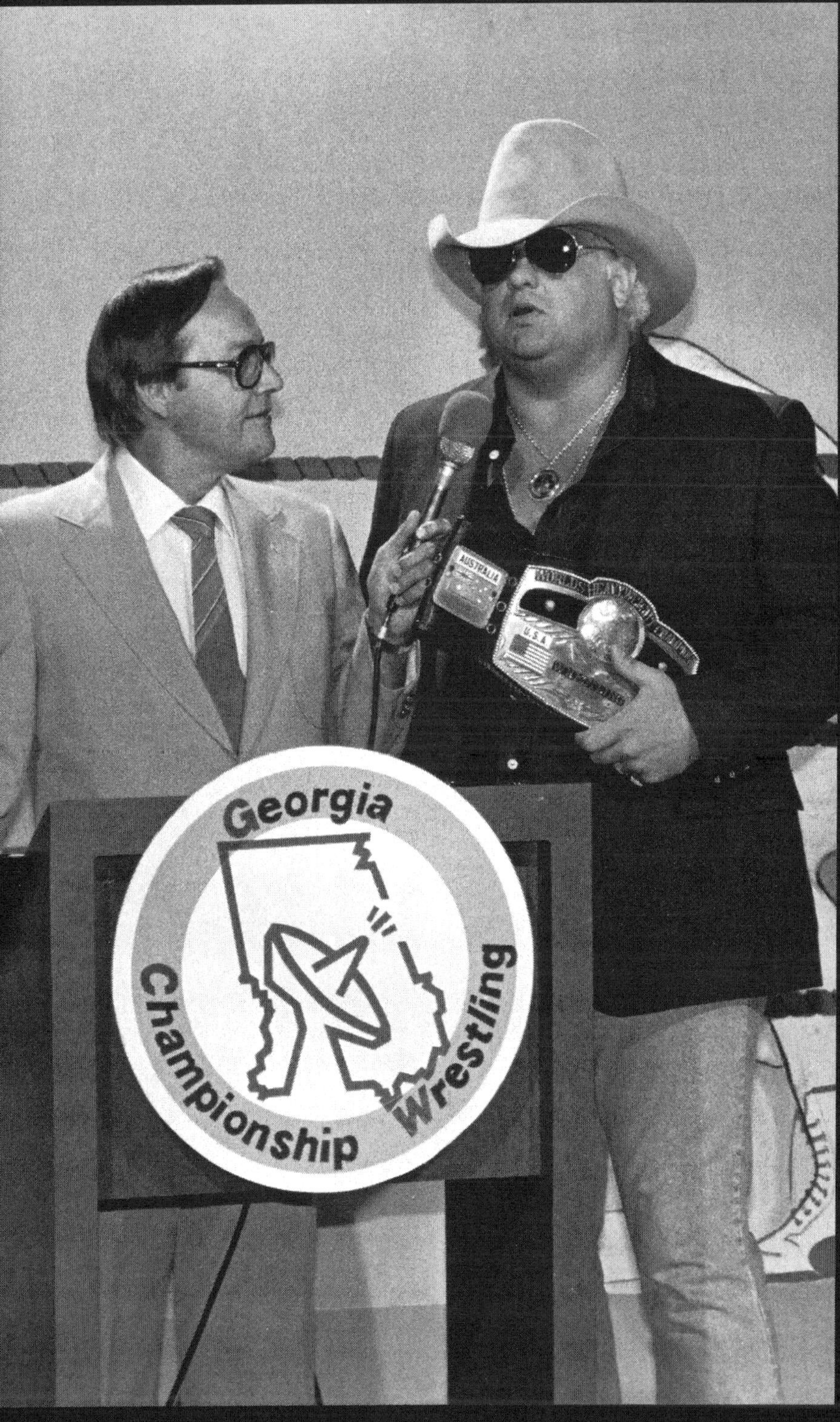
Georgia
Championship
Wrestling
AUSTRALIA
U.S.A.

THE RINGSIDER

GEORGIA'S OFFICIAL WRESTLING WEEKLY

VOL. 81   NO. 8

$1.00

IT HAPPENED HERE IN GEORGIA!
FOR THE FIRST TIME IN HISTORY !!
THE NWA WORLD'S HEAVYWEIGHT TITLE CHANGED HANDS IN AUGUSTA, GA.

TOMMY "WILDFIRE" RICH
BECAME WORLD'S CHAMPION! HARLEY RACE LATER REGARDED THE CROWN
TO BECOME A 6 TIMES WORLD CHAMPION !

"WILDFIRE" TOMMY RICH

Tommy "Wildfire" Rich held the NWA World Heavyweight Championship for four days in the spring of 1981, defeating Harley Race in Augusta, GA, on a Monday night and dropping the title back to Race in Gainesville, GA, on Friday of the same week.

Rich was one of the most well known wrestlers of the era, riding an enormous wave of popularity off of the top rated *Georgia Championship Wrestling* television program seen nationwide on the cable Superstation WTBS out of Atlanta. He was nevertheless a controversial choice as champion. His reign was similar to the short term title runs of Shohei Baba and Dusty Rhodes before him in that they were not planned succession changes by the NWA board, but rather gestures of goodwill to a member promoter, in this case Georgia promoter Jim Barnett, who was also an officer in the NWA. It is doubtful that the full board approved this change.

All indications were that Race and Barnett made a deal for the short-term title change to elevate business in the territory while elevating Tommy Rich as well. Fans everywhere suddenly believed that the NWA title could change hands on any given night in any town, large or small. They had just seen it happen with Tommy Rich.

While critics write off Rich's five day title reign as almost a footnote in NWA title history, Race himself dispels that notion. When speaking of the event on a documentary interview, Race firmly asserted that regardless of the length of the reign or the circumstances under which it took place, Rich pinned him cleanly and carried the title, and as such earned the right to be called and remembered as NWA World Heavyweight Champion.

"NATURE BOY" RIC FLAIR

Ric Flair is generally regarded as the greatest NWA world champion of all time. No better endorsement could come in that regard than when Harley Race hugged Ric Flair and told him so during Flair's emotional farewell after Wrestlemania in 2008.

From the first months after Flair began his pro wrestling career in Minnesota in 1972, he knew he wanted to eventually rise to the top of his chosen profession. As he related in a 2000 interview on television, that desire became an obsession when he first laid eyes on the NWA championship belt. Flair had moved to Charlotte, NC, and had begun his climb to stardom competing in the Mid-Atlantic Wrestling territory. Jack Brisco was defending the NWA title on a hot summer night in Greenville, SC and a young Ric Flair was wrestling on the card as well. Ric got his first close look at the belt in the locker room that night and knew then his one goal was to eventually wear it.

Over the next few years, Flair would continue to work hard and gain experience. He got his first notoriety in national newsstand magazines in 1976 during a year long feud with Wahoo McDaniel over the Mid-Atlantic heavyweight championship. That same year, he got himself booked in Madison Square Garden for the WWWF. Flair began making appearances in the Florida and Georgia territories in 1977 and 1978 as promoters around the country were beginning to take notice.

The first indication that he was being considered as a potential candidate to be NWA champion was when St. Louis promoter Sam Muchnick, the former and long time president of the NWA and one of the sport's top power brokers, began booking him on his big cards at the Kiel Auditorium in 1978. A wrestler who wanted to be NWA champion had to impress and do well for

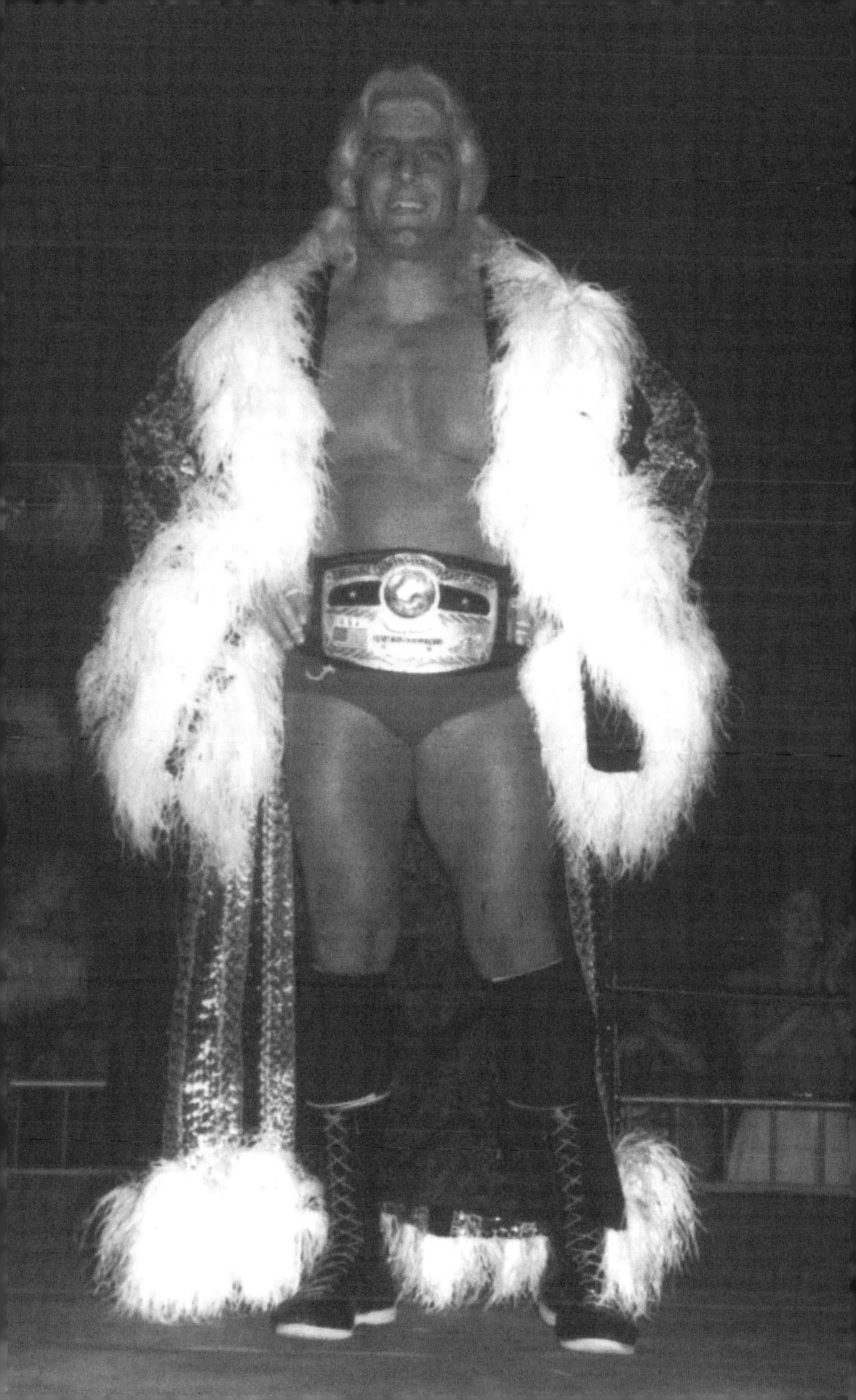

Mr. Muchnick. Not long after his initial St. Louis appearances, Flair's name started coming up at annual NWA board meetings as a candidate for champion.

In September of 1981 in Kansas City, Flair's dream finally came true when he defeated Dusty Rhodes to win his first world championship and strapped the Ten Pounds of Gold around his waist. In those days, this was the greatest honor you could receive in the business. NWA member promoters put their trust in, and placed their bets for success on, the Nature Boy.

Flair would not let them down. He drew huge houses for promoters across the United States and around the globe. His schedule alone (as with other champions as well) might kill the average man, defending the title and appearing in a different city nearly every night of the year for a decade as NWA champion.

NWA promoters gave Flair the title a second time in 1983

when he defeated Harley Race at the first Starrcade event in Greensboro. Starrcade was the forerunner for Wrestlemania and all the big shows that followed over the years. Flair has said that this second win may have been more special than the first since it reaffirmed the NWA member promoters' confidence in him and also because it took place in his home territory. It was the first time the world title had changed hands in front of Mid-Atlantic wrestling fans, and those fans were delighted to see their hometown hero be the one to take it there.

Flair won the title many times, eventually breaking Harley Race's record of eight NWA world title reigns. Depending on how you count them, he would win over 16 world championships. He carried the torch during a revolutionary period in the business when the advent of national cable television, among other factors, led to the stronger territorial promoters going national and the weaker promoters being swallowed up or going out of business all together. In this manner, Flair not only dominated wrestling as the champion of a territorial system, but also lead pro wrestling as one of its top performers on a competitive national stage.

A weekly platform on a highly rated national cable broadcast as well as a powerful syndicated network helped Flair establish the Ten Pounds of Gold as one of the most recognized championship belts of them all. It was an iconic symbol not only in the United States but in pro wrestling worldwide, especially in Japan where promoter Shohei Baba's use of the champion and the prominent position of the title belt itself, helped establish it as the top trophy there as well.

Flair's career spans nearly five decades and is now entering its fifth, as the Nature Boy shows no signs of slowing down. He is and forever will be "the man" to generations of wrestling fans.

"I'm a kiss stealin', wheelin' dealin', limosine ridin', jet flyin', son of a gun.

I wear around my waist the most coveted trophy in all of professional sports: the Ten Pounds of Gold, the world heavyweight championship.

There's only one."

- Ric Flair
National Television
April 1985

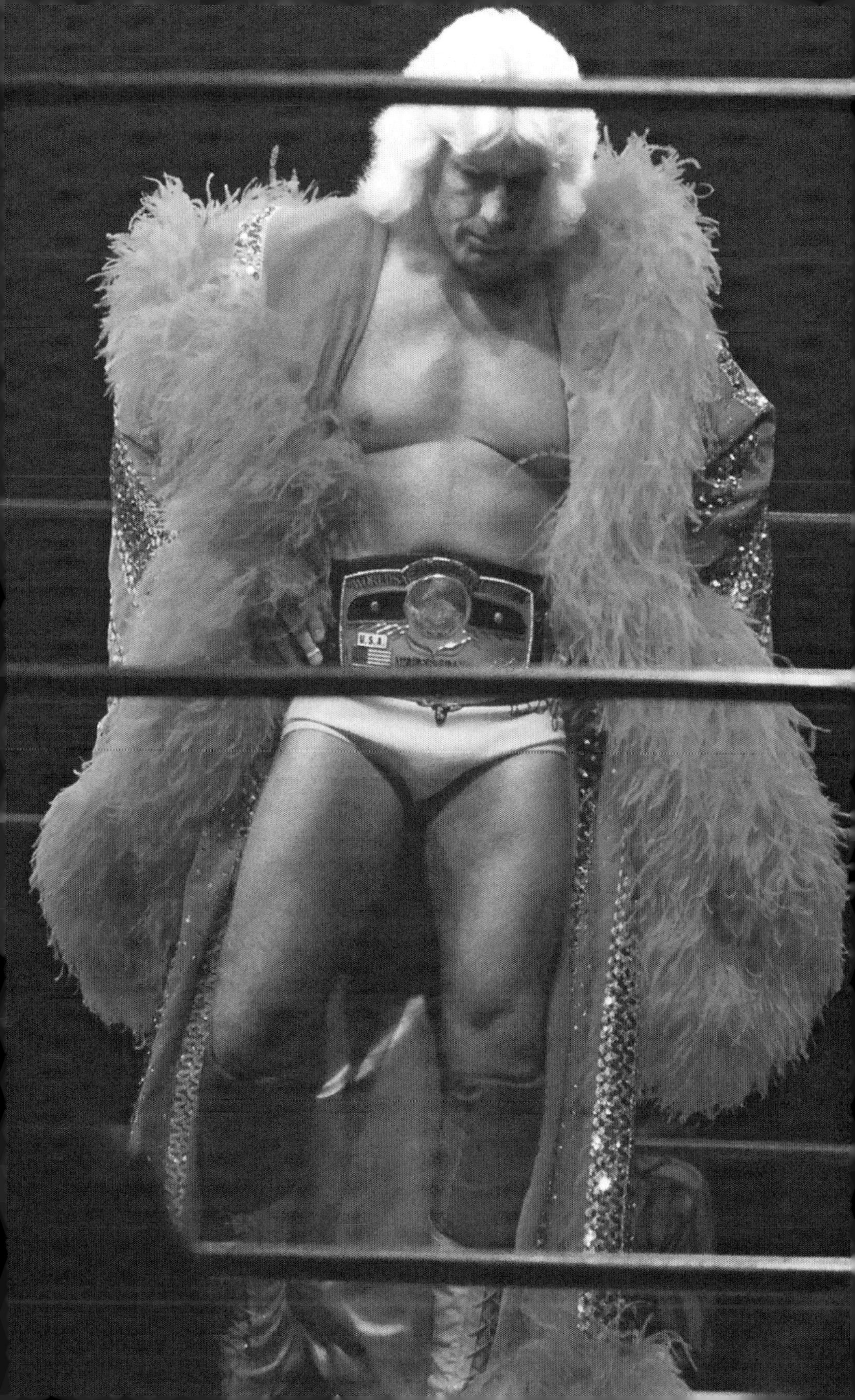
U.S.A.

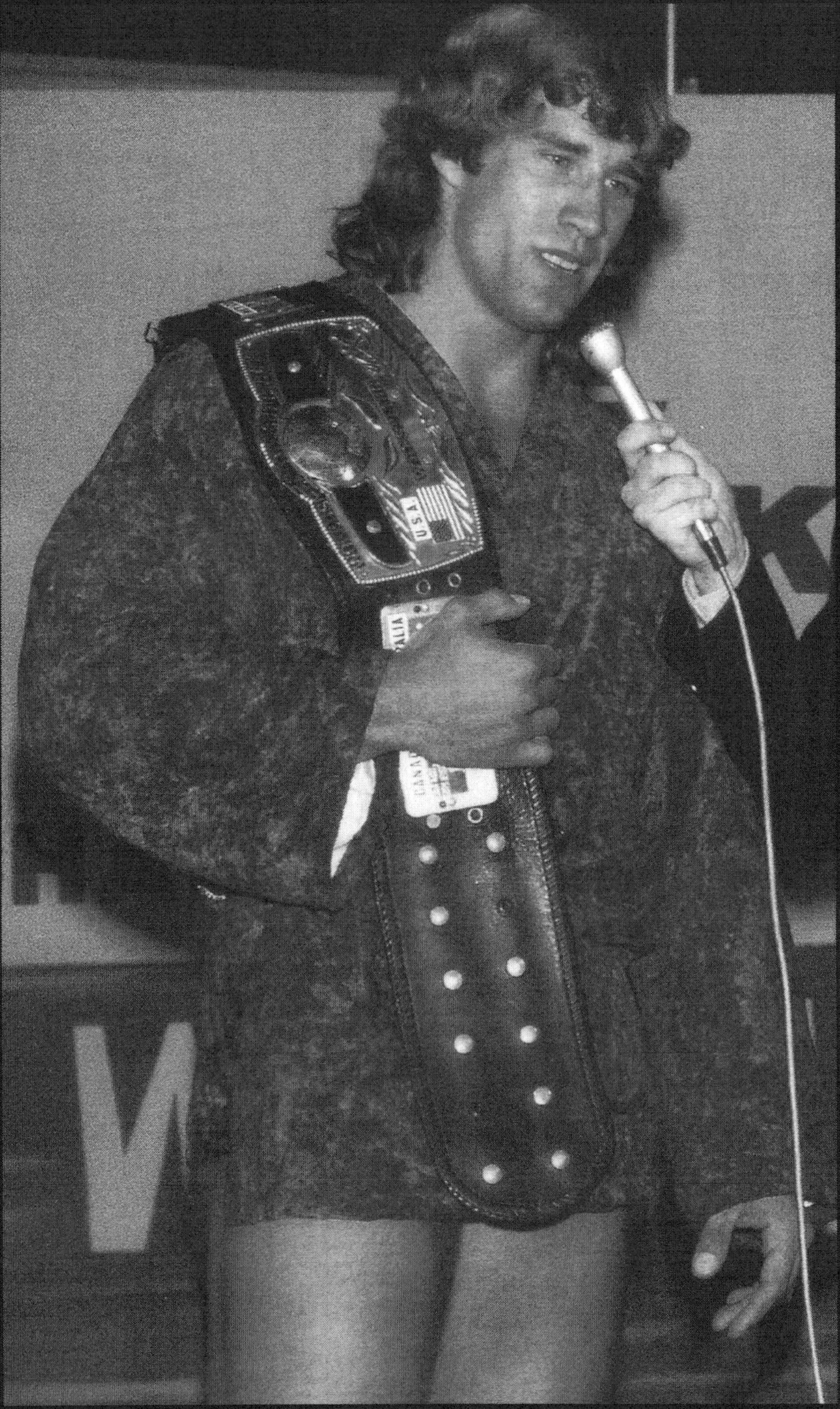
U.S.A

KERRY VON ERICH

Kerry Von Erich won the NWA World Championship in one of the most dramatic and bittersweet stories ever told in pro-wrestling. While some critics have branded that story the exploitation of a brother's death, the true account falls somewhere in between.

On May 5, 1984 in front of over 32,000 fans in Texas Stadium, Kerry upset Ric Flair to win the title in a match dedicated to the memory of his brother David who had died a few months earlier. As the story was told, it should have been (and by all accounts eventually would have been) David winning the title, as he was one of several leading candidates to be made champion by the NWA promoters during that time. If it were some great work of fiction or some great script written for the silver screen, it might just have been the greatest Texas wrestling story ever told.

Except sadly, this story was true.

But suspending disbelief, it was the perfect story, and the imagery was off the charts. Moments after winning the championship, Kerry stood in the center of the ring and held the NWA belt, a yellow rose, and the state flag of Texas high over his head. Throw in the beautiful blue robe honoring David that

The initials "KVE" can be seen scratched into the main plate of the belt.

Kerry wore to the ring and you have a treasure of images from that day that are simply timeless, and are a fabled part of NWA championship lore.

Kerry would only hold the title a few short weeks. He loved the idea of being champion so much, and evidently lamented having to give it up so soon, that he lightly scratched his initials into the main plate of the belt (seen above), a mark that went unnoticed for many years.

In fact, it's hardly noticeable at all. So much so that Ric Flair himself was unaware the mark was there, even though he has had the belt in his possession since it was retired in 1986. In order to get it to show up in photos we had to try positioning our lights at different angles, finally successfully illuminating the scratches. Moving the lights or repositioning the belt even slightly would often result in the mark disappearing in photos.

The mark shows up in several of the photos in this book, including the cover shot.

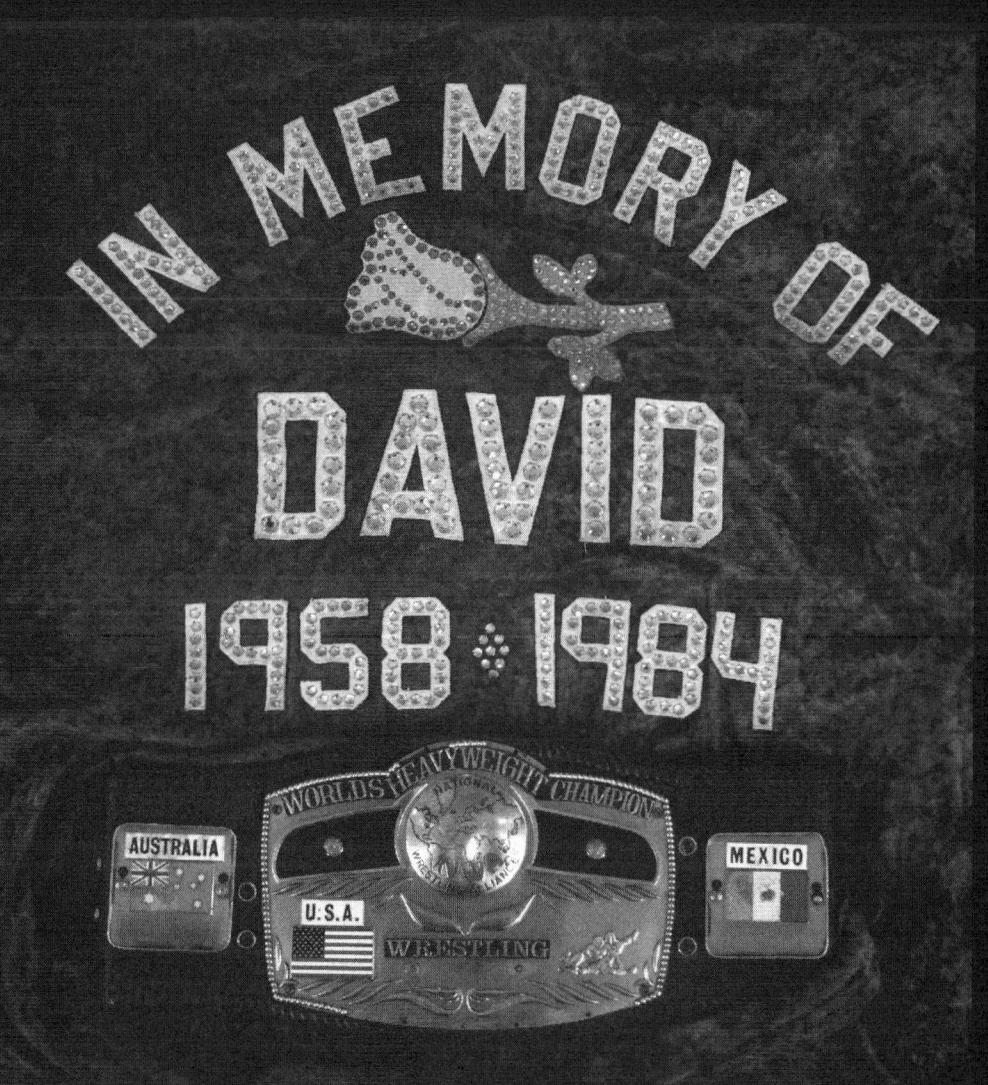

The Ten Pounds of Gold with the ring jacket Kerry Von Erich wore in Texas Stadium when he defeated Ric Flair in May of 1984.

THE FLARE FO
HARLEY RACE
AUSTRALIA
U.S.A.
PHOT
PRO Wrestling ILLUSTRATED
Exclusive Coverage
Ric Flair Whips Harley Race For The NWA Title:
A SECOND CHANCE AT GREATNESS
Tommy Rich's War With Ted DiBiase: FOR GLORY OR REVENGE?
The Real Story Behind The Hogan-Andre Tag: WHO WILL TURN ON THE OTHER FIRST?
THE MAN WHO SACRIFICED STARDOM TO SAVAGE J.J. DILLON
AGAZINE
UME 4, NO. 8
$3.00
Giant, Full-Color Pinup of KING JERRY
別冊ゴング
10
●レイスからローデスそして再びレイスへ
NWA世界王座交代劇の全貌
8・28夢のオールスター戦総括!!
EXCLUSIVE PHOTOS:
PIPER & ORNDORFF'S BRUTAL BATTLE AGAINST JOHNSON & ATLAS
VICTORY SPORTS SERIES
THE Wrestler
Kerry Von Erich Wins The NWA World Title:
FOR DAVID . . . FOR TEXAS . . . FOR WRESTLING!
RIC FLAIR: KERRY'S JUST BORROWING MY BELT!
GIANT FULL-COLOR PINUP OF RODDY PIPER
PRO Wrestling ILLUSTRAT
PRESS CONFER
HARLEY RA
"I've Proved I'm The Bes
The Fans Make It Offic
BRUNO SAMMARTINO NAMED GREATES WWF CHAMPION EVER
Mil Mascaras & Tito Santana:
HOW THE PERFECT TAG TEAM WAS FORMED
Revealed:
PAUL ELLERING'S PLOT TO BRAINWASH ARN ANDERSON
R PINUP OF RANDY SAVAGE
WORLD CLASS WRESTLING
November 1985
Wrestling ILLUSTRAT
別冊ゴング
9
ワイド特集 激動のNWA新王者はジャック!
別冊9月号 ¥280
2人のジョニーが来襲!
ワールド・シリーズ展望
NWA総会が投げた波紋
NEW N.W.A. WORLD CHAMPION
JACK BRISCO
nwa WRESTLING magazine
Volume I No. 1
The Official Publication Of The National Wrestling Alliance
CONGRATULATED
and Co-Promoter
NGSID
OF THE CHAMPION"
TES . . .
'S CHAMPION

Chapter Seven
Spanning the Globe:
NWA World Title Changes 1973-1984
A Title History of the Ten Pounds of Gold

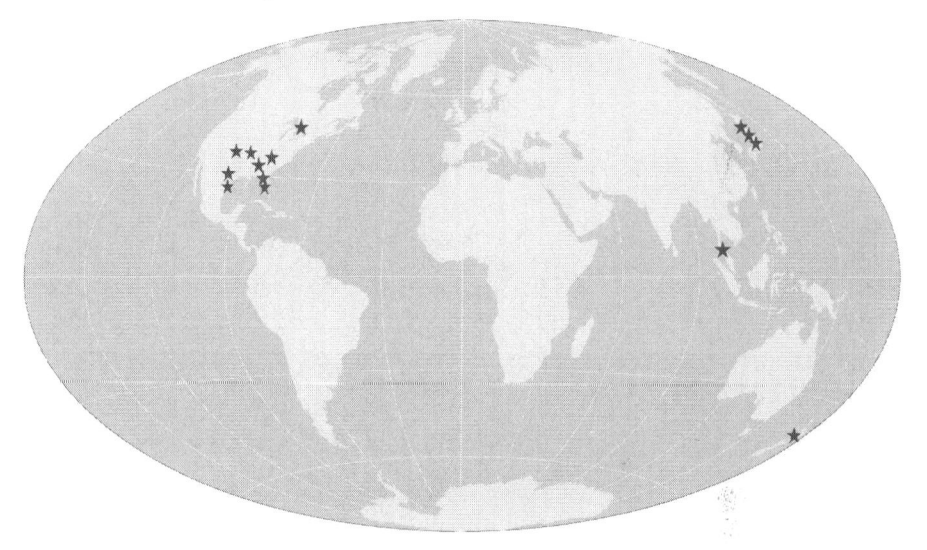

During the years that the domed-globe belt was defended, it saw many title changes that took place in five different countries around the globe. Factoring in locations and impact on various organizations and territories, the Ten Pounds of Gold version of the NWA title in the 1970s and 1980s was truly more of a world championship trophy than any other wrestling title before or since.

The following pages summarize those changes and also provide a glimpse behind the scenes to the circumstances that led up to each one.

Friday, July 20, 1973
Harley Race receives new NWA championship Belt
Gulf Athletic Club (Houston Wrestling)

Harley Race had defeated Dory Funk, Jr. for the NWA title on March 24, 1972 at Memorial Hall in Kansas City, KS. He proudly wore the version of the NWA title that Thesz, Rogers, O'Conner and Kiniski had all worn before him.

Race would be the last person to step through the ropes wearing that belt. On July 20 at the Sam Houston Coliseum in Houston, TX, NWA President Sam Muchnick presented him with a brand new championship belt before his title defense against Jack Brisco. This version of the belt would come to be known as the Ten Pounds of Gold, and Race will always be remembered as the first person to wear and defend it.

Friday, July 20, 1973
Jack Brisco defeats Harley Race
Gulf Athletic Club (Houston Wrestling)
Houston, Texas

When Dory Funk, Jr. had made the decision to step down, the NWA board of directors chose Jack Brisco to be the next champion. Others in consideration were Harley Race and Terry Funk.

It took place a few months later than originally planned but Brisco won the NWA world championship on July 20, 1973 at the Sam Houston Coliseum in Houston, TX, defeating Race by taking the 2nd and 3rd falls of a two-out-of-three falls match. In doing so, he became the first person to win the Ten Pounds of Gold version of the belt.

The referee was longtime wrestler Bronko Lubich, who was recently retired from active competition and had become an NWA official. Also in attendance was NWA President Sam Muchnick to present a new championship belt to Race before the match.

Cover of GONG Magazine in Japan reporting the new NWA World Champion Jack Brisco. The issue had over a half dozen features and articles on Brisco's career and historic win in Houston.

For detailed information on the Race/Brisco match, including the build-up and results, see the earlier chapter "Houston, Texas: The Birth of the Belt" on page 19.

Friday, December 2, 1974
Shohei Giant Baba defeats Jack Brisco
All Japan Pro Wrestling
Kagoshima, Japan

According to Jack Brisco in his autobiography, Terry Funk approached him about an offer from Giant Baba to let Baba briefly win the NWA title when Brisco was scheduled to tour Japan. In exchange, Baba would pay Brisco $10,000 cash.

At that time, wrestlers chosen to be NWA champion by its board were required to post a $25,000 security bond before getting the title. The bond would be held in escrow until that wrestler lost the title to the next champion at which time the $25,000 would be returned to him.

Brisco was nervous about doing a short-term change because it might violate the terms of the bond agreement. He told Funk to go back to Baba with his counter offer which was that he receive $25,000 from Baba, an amount equal to the security deposit. Brisco also would inform president Sam Muchnick and the board of directors of the title change in advance. Baba agreed. While Muchnick and the board weren't thrilled with the idea, Brisco wrote that they did not object.

Brisco took former NWA champion Pat O'Conner with him on the trip as his second and to act somewhat as an enforcer and look out for his interests.

The match was a 2-of-3 falls contest. Baba won the first with a Russian leg-sweep. Brisco took the second with his figure-four leg lock. Baba won the third and deciding fall at 3:30 of that fall after a flying clothesline.

Friday, December 9, 1974
Jack Brisco defeats Shohei Giant Baba
All Japan Pro Wrestling
Toyohashi, Japan

After one successful defense by Baba in a rematch, Jack Brisco regained the NWA championship on December 9, 1974 at the Civic Center in Toyohashi, Japan.

Baba won the first fall with a back breaker. Brisco took the second with the figure four leglock. Brisco regained the title with a tip of the hat to Pat O'Conner by pinning Baba with the "O'Conner rollup" to regain the NWA title.

Brisco recounts in his book about the ordeal of getting his $25,000 back to the U.S. He was paid in cash, and regulations were that he could not take more than $5000 cash back to the U.S. He decided to smuggle it back in, taping the bundles of cash to his stomach and legs. He made the complete flight from Japan to Hawaii and finally back to St. Louis with $25,000 cash taped to his body.

Wednesday, December 10, 1975
Terry Funk defeats Jack Brisco
Championship Wrestling from Florida
Miami Beach, Florida

In the spring of 1975, becoming weary of the travel the championship required, Jack Brisco notified the NWA that he was ready to step down as champion. At the annual NWA convention held in August of that year in New Orleans, LA, the NWA board settled on two men as the leading contenders to succeed Brisco – Terry Funk and former champion Harley Race.

Funk's father was pushing hard for his younger son to get the strap, no doubt enamored of the prospects of having both his sons Dory Jr. and Terry be the only brothers to hold the NWA title. Bob Geigel pushed hard for Harley Race. By the time of the NWA convention in New Orleans in August, the board was evenly split between the two and it would be up to the new president of the

NWA to break the tie.

The National Wrestling Alliance was going through many changes during this time, not the least of which was long time NWA president Sam Muchnick stepping down from those responsibilities and Texas promoter Jack Adkisson (Fritz Von Erich) assuming that leadership role. In his first major decision as president, Adkisson cast the deciding vote for Funk, and the date and location for the title change was set for December 10, 1975 in Miami Beach, Florida.

In a classic bait-and-switch angle, the main event that night was billed as Brisco defending against former champion Dory Funk, Jr., but when Junior couldn't be there, Terry Funk challenged Brisco in his place. (For more details, see the earlier Terry Funk profile on page 89.)

Funk defeated Brisco in a one-fall match, capturing him in a cradle when Brisco was attempting to apply the figure four leglock.

It was a bittersweet moment for Funk as his father wasn't able to see his dream realized of both sons winning the title. Dory Funk, Sr. had passed away a few months earlier.

The tape of the match sent to the territories was voiced over by long time Florida TV commentator Gordon Solie, and was notable for the mixed use of slow motion footage during playback of the match, which added a somewhat cinematic feel to the clip.

Sunday, February 6, 1977
Harley Race defeats Terry Funk
Toronto Maple Leaf Wrestling
Toronto, Canada

Harley Race could be forgiven for thinking by 1975 he may have been snake bit by destiny in his hopes of having an extended run as NWA champion. When the 1973 planned title switch from Dory Funk Jr. to Jack Brisco fell through due to Dory's accident, Race was chosen as the transitional champion to later defeat Dory

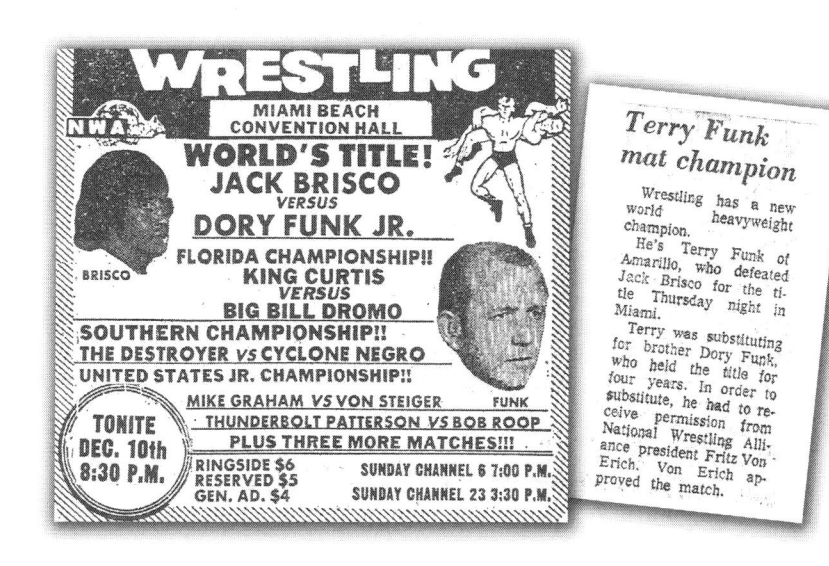

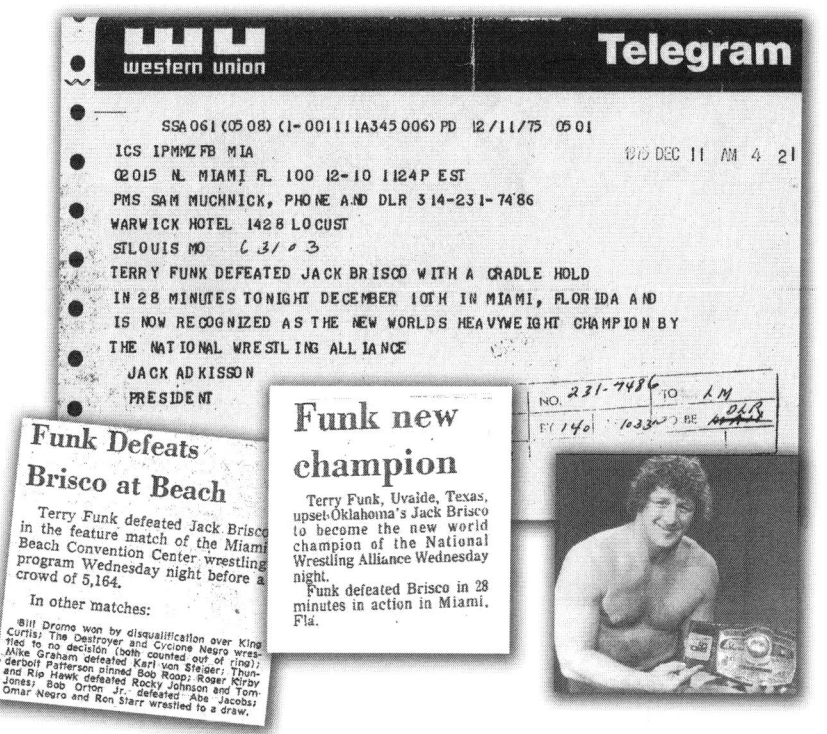

Above: Memorabilia of Terry Funk's title win over Jack Brisco at Convention Hall, including the telegram Sam Muchnick sent on behalf of NWA President Jack Adkisson. Notice the newspaper ad for the show billed Brisco defending against Dory Funk, Jr., which was the promoted main event. Terry substituted for his older brother and went on to upset Brisco for the belt.

115

NWA Champ Harley Race and the Ten Pounds of Gold on "The Ringsider", the event publication of Georgia Championship Wrestling.

and then drop the title to Brisco. While it was an honor to be given the NWA title for any amount of time, Race wasn't interested in history recording him as merely a transitional champion.

When Brisco decided to give up the title in 1975, it was assumed by many within the NWA that Race would be the natural choice to succeed him. Race had done well in the two months he had previously held the title, and was enthusiastically supported by sponsor Bob Geigel and others. But a political battle ensued with Dory Funk, Sr. convincing enough of the board, including new president and fellow Texan Jack Adkisson, to give Terry Funk the title instead.

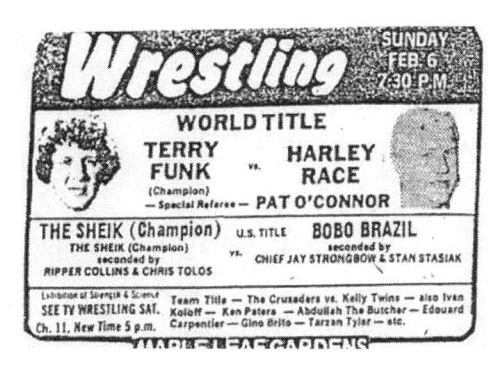

Race's patience was rewarded, however, when Terry Funk was ready to drop the title and the NWA board overwhelmingly chose Race as his successor.

Toronto's Maple Leaf Gardens was chosen as the site for early 1977. Promoter Frank Tunney set the date for February 6, and Race defeated Funk with an Indian Death Lock at 14:10 of a one-fall match.

TV commentators for the match included former NWA world champion "Whipper" Billy Watson and former NWA president Sam Muchnick. Former NWA champion Pat O'Conner was originally billed to be the special referee for the match, but was replaced by one of the local area officials. Toronto ring announcer Norm Kimber made a particularly dramatic announcement of the win following Race's historic victory.

Harley Race was now a 2-time champion, and on his way to becoming one of the most respected, well traveled, and long reigning champions in NWA history.

Tuesday, August 21, 1979
Dusty Rhodes defeated Harley Race
Championship Wrestling from Florida
Tampa, Florida

Sunday, August 26, 1979
Harley Race regained title from Dusty Rhodes
Orlando, Florida

Dusty Rhodes had become one of the most popular wrestlers in pro-wrestling in the late 1970s, and had become a huge attraction in many of the various NWA territories, as well as the WWWF. His primary sponsor for the title was Florida promoter Eddie Graham, who by 1979 had great sway within the Alliance and had been its president from 1976-1978. Graham lobbied hard for Dusty to be made champion, but Rhodes was not in the same mold as the long lineage of champions that came before. But following the retirement of Sam Muchnick as president in 1975, promoters had slowly begun to look at things differently, stepping outside the traditional ideas of what the NWA champion should look like. The first manifestation of this was the selection of the rowdy Terry Funk as champion that same year. Rhodes was a similar choice, and there was no denying Rhodes was a huge draw everywhere he went.

The NWA decided to reward Graham and Rhodes with a short-term title switch in Florida that would be both a boost to Rhodes's stature within the NWA and a favor to business in Graham's territory, but would not be a change in long-term title succession.

Rhodes won the NWA title on August 21, 1979 at the Fort Homer Hesterly Armory in Tampa, FL, dropping it back to Race five days later on August 26 at the Sports Stadium in Orlando. Part of the angle to get the title back to Race was former champion and Rhodes nemesis Terry Funk injuring Rhodes in advance of the Orlando rematch.

Fans by and large outside of Florida did not learn of the title change until it was reported in the news-stand wrestling magazines months later.

Wednesday, October 31, 1979
Shohei Baba defeated Harley Race
All Japan Pro Wrestling
Nagoya, Japan

Wednesday, November 7, 1979
Harley Race regained title from Shohei Baba
Amagasaki, Japan

Thursday, September 4, 1980
Shohei Baba defeated Harley Race
Saga, Japan

Wednesday, September 10, 1980
Harley Race regained title from Shohei Baba
Ohtsu, Japan

In much the same manner as with Jack Brisco back in 1974, and for most of the same reasons, Giant Baba defeated Harley Race twice in Japan to win the NWA title, for a week each time, in 1979 and 1980.

The short title runs were aimed at elevating business in Japan and helping Baba keep a competitive edge over his promotional rival Antonio Inoki. For more information, see the earlier profile on Shohei "Giant" Baba on page 87.)

These title changes were not voted on or approved by the NWA board, and Race maintains they were favors to his good friend Baba. Reportedly, following the 1979 change, Inoki brought footage of the match to the next annual NWA board meeting in hopes of raising some issue regarding its impropriety, but the NWA board basically shrugged it shoulders. Race and Baba repeated the whole ordeal a few months later in 1980.

Much like the 5-day title switch with Rhodes in Florida, fans in the U.S. weren't aware of these changes until they read about them in the wrestling magazines.

Monday, April 27, 1981
Tommy Rich defeated Harley Race
Georgia Championship Wrestling
Augusta, GA

Friday, May 1, 1981
Harley Race regained the title from Tommy Rich
Gainesville, GA

Like the title exchanges Race had with Dusty Rhodes and Giant Baba in 1979 and 1980, another short term exchange took place in 1981 for booker Jim Barnett and Georgia Championship Wrestling.

Tommy "Wildfire" Rich upset Race at the Bell Auditorium in Augusta GA, a town more notable in sports circles as the home of the Masters Golf Championship. Race went for a vertical suplex, but Rich floated over his shoulders and then caught Race out of nowhere with the "Thesz press", one of Rich's signature finishing maneuvers. Four days later on a Friday night in Gainesville GA, Race regained the title.

The next day on the nationally televised "Georgia Championship Wrestling" program on cable Superstation WTBS, the world learned of the title change and footage was shown of Rich's win in Augusta. NWA president Jim Crockett, Jr. had ironically been in Japan when Rich won the title, and as the story goes, flew back to appear on the Georgia show with the new champion, only to learn as he landed that Race had regained the title the night before.

This title exchange was not voted on or approved by the full NWA board, in the same fashion as the previous short-term switches.

Sunday, June 21, 1981
Dusty Rhodes defeated Harley Race
Georgia Championship Wrestling
Atlanta, GA

As wrestling moved into the 1980s, "The American Dream" Dusty Rhodes remained as popular as he had been through the second half of the 1970s, and was more politically connected than ever.

The NWA board decided to end Race's tenure as champion and the nod was given to Rhodes. On June 21, 1981 in the Omni Arena in Atlanta, he defeated Race with a flying body-press from the top turnbuckle. NWA President Jim Crockett was in attendance.

The match was taped and most of it aired on Superstation WTBS, called by Gordon Solie. Rhodes would only hold the title a few months.

September 17, 1981
Ric Flair defeated Dusty Rhodes
Heart of America Promotions
Kansas City, KS

Ric Flair's name first came up as a potential candidate for the NWA championship when sponsor Jim Crockett, Jr. started getting him booked into St. Louis for promoter Sam Muchnick in 1978. Muchnick liked what he saw and from that moment forward, Flair was eyed as a possible successor down the road. Flair was booked into Madison Square Garden for the WWWF around the same time. Flair had drawn well in Georgia and Florida, even taking the Crockett version of the U.S. championship into those territories. He was a big draw in St. Louis, too, and at that point it wasn't a matter of "if", but "when".

Flair's time finally came when he met Dusty Rhodes on neutral ground at Memorial Hall in Kansas City, KS, for promoter Bob Geigel on Thursday, September 17, 1981. The special referee

Ric Flair holds the NWA world championship high in the air moments after defeating Dusty Rhodes in Kansas City, KS, September 17, 1981

assigned for the match was legendary 6-time former NWA champion Lou Thesz. Jim Crockett, Jr. was in the ring when both Flair and Rhodes were introduced. Larry Matysik voiced over the video sent to all the territories.

Flair had weakened the legs of Rhodes with his figure four leglock at several points during the match. Rhodes attempted a vertical suplex on Flair, but his legs gave out and Flair fell on top of him for the three count at 23:54 of a one fall contest.

Thesz handed the Ten Pounds of Gold to Flair, and one of the great championship runs was underway.

Friday, June 10, 1983
Harley Race defeated Ric Flair
St. Louis Wrestling Club
St. Louis, MO

Harley Race made history on June 10, 1983 in his hometown of St. Louis when he pinned Ric Flair to win the NWA world heavyweight championship for a record breaking seventh time, eclipsing the record previously held by Lou Thesz.

In an awkward finish, Flair had delivered a back suplex to Race and held him in place for the pin when Race lifted his shoulder at the count of three. The referee ruled that Flair's shoulders were also on the mat and by virtue of that, Race had actually scored the pinfall on Flair.

In reality, Race's final run as champion (save for his later two-day stint in the Far East) was largely brought about by a promotional battle for the city of St. Louis after the retirement of longtime NWA president Sam Muchnick. But it also allowed for the build-up for Flair to get the title back at one of the biggest shows ever, the inaugural Starrcade event.

Race hit the ground running like he had never lost the championship to begin with, defending the title in all corners of the globe along the way. His final big run was perhaps his best.

Thursday, November 24, 1983
Ric Flair regained the title from Harley Race
Mid-Atlantic Wrestling / Jim Crockett Promotions
Greensboro, NC

It was a masterful build-up to a championship title change and led to one of the most successfully promoted events in the history of the business at that time.

Ric Flair began his chase to regain the NWA world championship almost as soon as he lost it, aggressively pursuing Race not only in his Mid-Atlantic home territory but also back in St. Louis where Race had just regained the belt in June, 1983. Flair won a tournament for the Missouri heavyweight title, a title vacated by Race when he regained the world title. The Missouri title was known to be a stepping-stone to the NWA world championship and when Flair won that tournament (defeating David Von Erich in the finals) it was almost as if Flair was sending a message to Race and his home area: I'm coming to get my world belt back.

The story went that Race so feared Flair coming after him that he placed a $25,000 bounty on Flair, payable to anyone who would eliminate Flair from wrestling. It almost worked, as Flair's friend Bob Orton, Jr. turned on Flair and severely injured him with the help of Dick Slater. Race paid the bounty. Flair soon announced his retirement from wrestling.

But only a few weeks later, he returned in dramatic fashion. The NWA would now force Race to defend against Flair, and in a press conference in Florida, it was announced that Jim Crockett had outbid other promoters for the right to host the rematch at an event dubbed "Starrcade 83: A Flare for the Gold."

Former NWA champion Pat O'Conner was assigned as special referee for the match, but Crockett protested citing Race's business ties with O'Conner. Former champion Gene Kiniski was then assigned to replace O'Conner which greatly upset Race, and the match was ordered to be held inside of a steel cage.

The match was beamed via closed circuit television to towns

VICTORY RIDE

Ric Flair, wearing the Ten Pounds of Gold he regained moments earlier from Harley Race at Starrcade '83, is carried around the ring on the shoulders of Angelo Mosca. Legendary Mid-Atlantic Wrestling veteran Johnny Weaver is seen with several others celebrating Flair's monumental win.
November 24, 1983 Greensboro NC

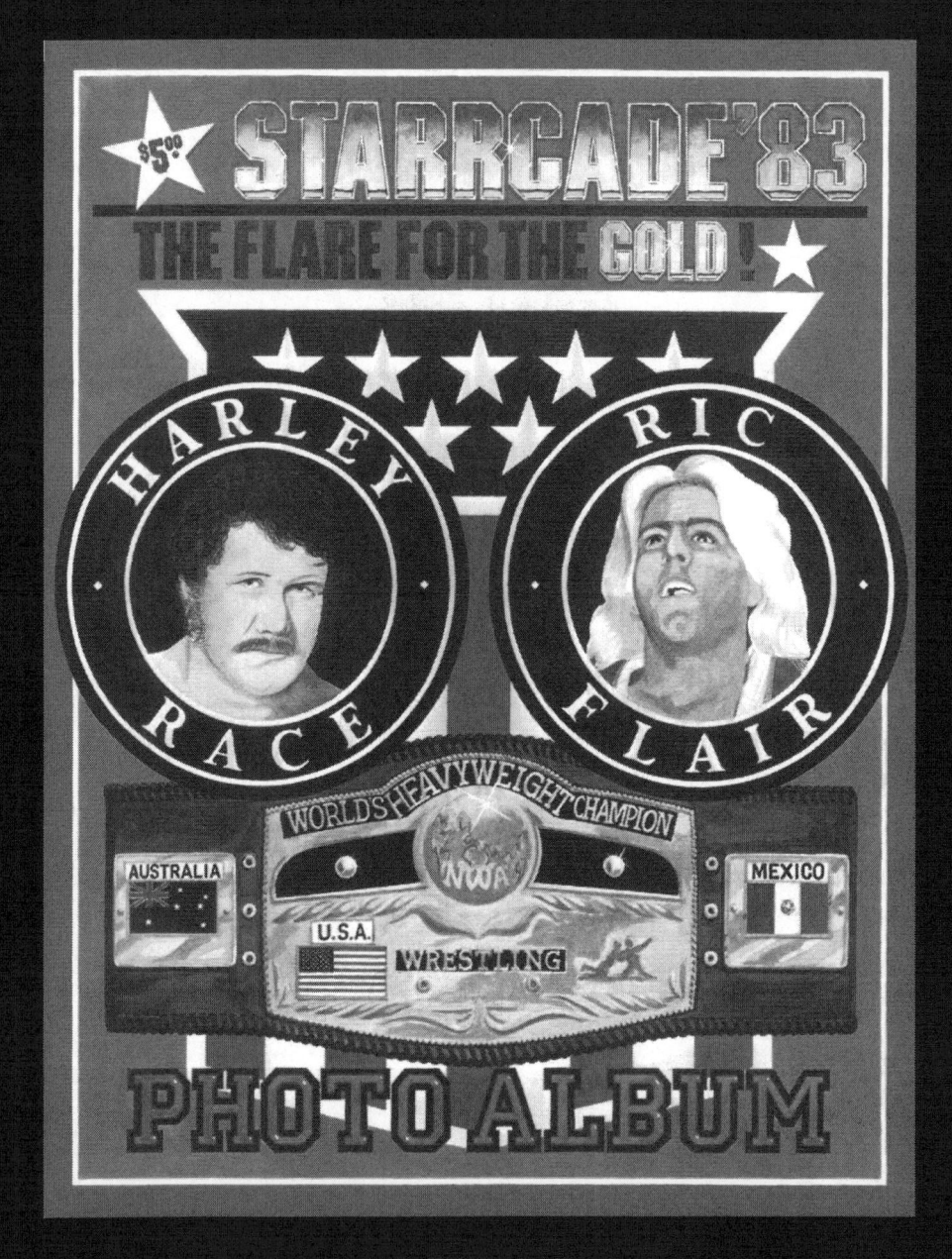

STARRCADE '83

One of Jim Crockett Promotions' most famous program covers. It was a throwback to the art covers of the mid-to-late 1970s that Les Thatcher produced for the promotion at the time. This one features an artist's rendition of NWA champion Harley Race and challenger Ric Flair along with a beautiful depiction of the Ten Pounds of Gold.

across the Mid-Atlantic territory as well as sites in Florida and Puerto Rico. It was to that point one of the largest combined gates in wrestling history. The event was called by Mid-Atlantic Wrestling broadcaster Bob Caudle and co-hosted by Gordon Solie.

Flair won the title when he hit Race with a flying body press off the top turnbuckle and referee Gene Kiniski made the historic three count.

Flair was extremely emotional in the ring after the match. He has said that this second NWA title win was more special than the first because it rekindled his self-confidence and demonstrated that the NWA promoters had faith in him to carry the title once again. It also didn't hurt that it took place in his home area in front of his fans.

Tuesday, March 20, 1984
Harley Race defeated Ric Flair*
New Zealand Pro-Wrestling Association
Wellington, New Zealand

Friday, March 23, 1984
NWA title returned to Ric Flair*
Kallang, Singapore
*These changes not officially recognized until many years later.

In what wound up being the final in a series of short-term title exchanges that began with Jack Brisco and Giant Baba in 1974, Flair and Race exchanged the title in New Zealand.

Promoter Steve Rickard arranged for the switch to help his local business. Race defeated Flair in New Zealand and then Flair reclaimed the title under unusual circumstances several days later in Singapore.

Some details surrounding these changes remain unclear even to this day. The only reporting in English known to have taken place was by the Wrestling Observer newsletter in the United States. Dave Meltzer reported in June of 1984 that Race had won the title on 3/21 in Auckland, New Zealand and lost the title back to Flair on 3/23 in Singapore. There was extensive reporting in the Japanese magazines following the tour, and brief notations in English accompanying two different articles point to Race winning the title in Wellington (not Auckland), New Zealand. A newspaper ad in the local papers confirms the date of the Wellington show as 3/20/84.

From translation of the Japanese reports, it appears the story presented there was that Race pinned Flair in Wellington on 3/20, but Flair claimed a fast count and appealed to the NWA through Paul Boesch as intermediary, who was on the tour. The NWA apparently returned the title to Flair on the first night of the three-date stretch (March 23-25) in Singapore, and Flair defeated Race on 3/24 at Geylang Stadium to secure the title.

With the title being returned to Flair, one might question the need to recognize these changes at all. However, various reports also show Race with possession of the belt and pinning Flair again in Auckland, New Zealand on 3/21 before going to Singapore, which could help justify recognizing his title win before being stripped of the title.

Sunday, May 6, 1984
Kerry Von Erich defeated Ric Flair
World Class Championship Wrestling
Irving, TX

Following the sudden and tragic death in February 1984 of David Von Erich, who at the time was thought to be a future candidate for the NWA championship, World Class Championship Wrestling organized a memorial show that would feature his younger brother, Kerry, challenging champion Ric Flair in David's memory.

The NWA approved a temporary switch to Kerry in a show of support to the family and the promotion, both reeling from the loss. Kerry defeated Flair with a backslide at 25:40 in a one fall contest held at the David Von Erich Memorial Parade of

Champions at Texas Stadium in Irving, Texas, just outside of Dallas.

Kerry assumed the dates already booked for the champion, and defended the title in Texas and then a tour through Florida before heading to Japan. (For more information on Kerry's emotional victory, see his profile on page 105.)

Thursday, May 24, 1984
Ric Flair regained title from Kerry Von Erich
All Japan Pro Wrestling
Yokosuka, Japan

Kerry Von Erich came to Japan and defended there against Jumbo Tsuruta before meeting Flair in a title rematch.

Flair regained the championship on May 24, 1984 in Yokosuka City, Japan in the third fall of a best 2-of-3 falls match when he reversed a roll up for the three count.

The title change between Flair and Kerry setup countless rematches between the two, a program that was so successful other promoters were booking the match into their territories as much as a year later.

Friday, February 14, 1986
Retirement of the "Domed Globe" Belt / Debut of "Big Gold" Belt
Orlando, FL

Unlike that special night in Houston in 1973, when Harley Race wore the old NWA belt into the ring for the last time, there was no special ceremony to retire the Ten Pounds of Gold. Sadly, it simply disappeared from the wrestling scene.

On February 14, 1986, Championship Wrestling from Florida held a special "Battle of the Belts II" event which was televised via satellite from Orlando to markets across the United States. On that card, Ric Flair defended the NWA world championship against Florida favorite Barry Windham who had just returned from the WWF. The evening had a special feel to it as Flair and Windham had developed a fierce rivalry in Florida in the early 1980s and their matches were magic. Fans hoped to see history made that night. They would, but probably not in they way they expected.

Just moments after Windham had made his way to the ring, the cameras cut away to Buddy Colt in the back who introduced NWA world champion Ric Flair.

"I thrive on being the greatest," Flair told Colt, "and to be the greatest, you have to wear something like this." And with that, Flair opened the robe he was wearing and displayed the brand new $35,000 gold and silver NWA world championship belt strapped securely around his waist.

While it was exciting to see the new belt and to be there when it was first defended, long time fans that recognized the Ten Pounds of Gold as the symbol and standard of excellence in the sport hated to see it disappear, especially without even a mention. Contrast this night with the night in Houston thirteen years earlier and the respect NWA President Sam Muchnick showed in retiring the belt worn by the likes of Thesz and O'Conner and presenting the new belt to Race and Brisco. One could only wish that the Ten Pounds of Gold had been shown the same respect on its way out as it had when it arrived.

NWA WORLD HEAVYWEIGHT CHAMPIONSHIP
DOMED GLOBE BELT - TITLE HISTORY

CHAMPION	DEFEATED	LOCATION	DATE
JACK BRISCO	HARLEY RACE	HOUSTON, TEXAS	07/20/73
SHOHEI BABA	JACK BRISCO	KAGOSHIMA, JAPAN	12/02/74
JACK BRISCO	SHOHEI BABA	TOYOHASHI, JAPAN	12/09/74
TERRY FUNK	JACK BRISCO	MIAMI BEACH, FLORIDA	12/10/75
HARLEY RACE	TERRY FUNK	TORONTO, CANADA	02/06/77
DUSTY RHODES	HARLEY RACE	TAMPA, FLORIDA	08/21/79
HARLEY RACE	DUSTY RHODES	ORLANDO, FLORIDA	08/26/79
SHOHEI BABA	HARLEY RACE	NAGOYA, JAPAN	10/31/79
HARLEY RACE	SHOHEI BABA	AMAGASAKI, JAPAN	11/07/79
SHOHEI BABA	HARLEY RACE	SAGA, JAPAN	09/04/80
HARLEY RACE	SHOHEI BABA	OHTSU, JAPAN	09/10/80
TOMMY RICH	HARLEY RACE	AUGUSTA, GEORGIA	04/27/81
HARLEY RACE	TOMMY RICH	GAINESVILLE, GEORGIA	05/01/81
DUSTY RHODES	HARLEY RACE	ATLANTA, GEORGIA	06/21/81
RIC FLAIR	DUSTY RHODES	KANSAS CITY, KANSAS	09/17/81
HARLEY RACE	RIC FLAIR	ST. LOUIS, MISSOURI	06/10/83
RIC FLAIR	HARLEY RACE	GREENSBORO, NC	11/24/83
HARLEY RACE*	RIC FLAIR	WELLINGTON, NEW ZEALAND	03/20/84
RIC FLAIR*	HARLEY RACE	KALLANG, SINGAPORE	03/23/84
KERRY VON ERICH	RIC FLAIR	IRVING, TEXAS	05/06/84
RIC FLAIR	KERRY VON ERICH	YOKOSUKA, JAPAN	05/24/84

* Title change not recognized by the National Wrestling Alliance until many years later.

AUSTRALIA

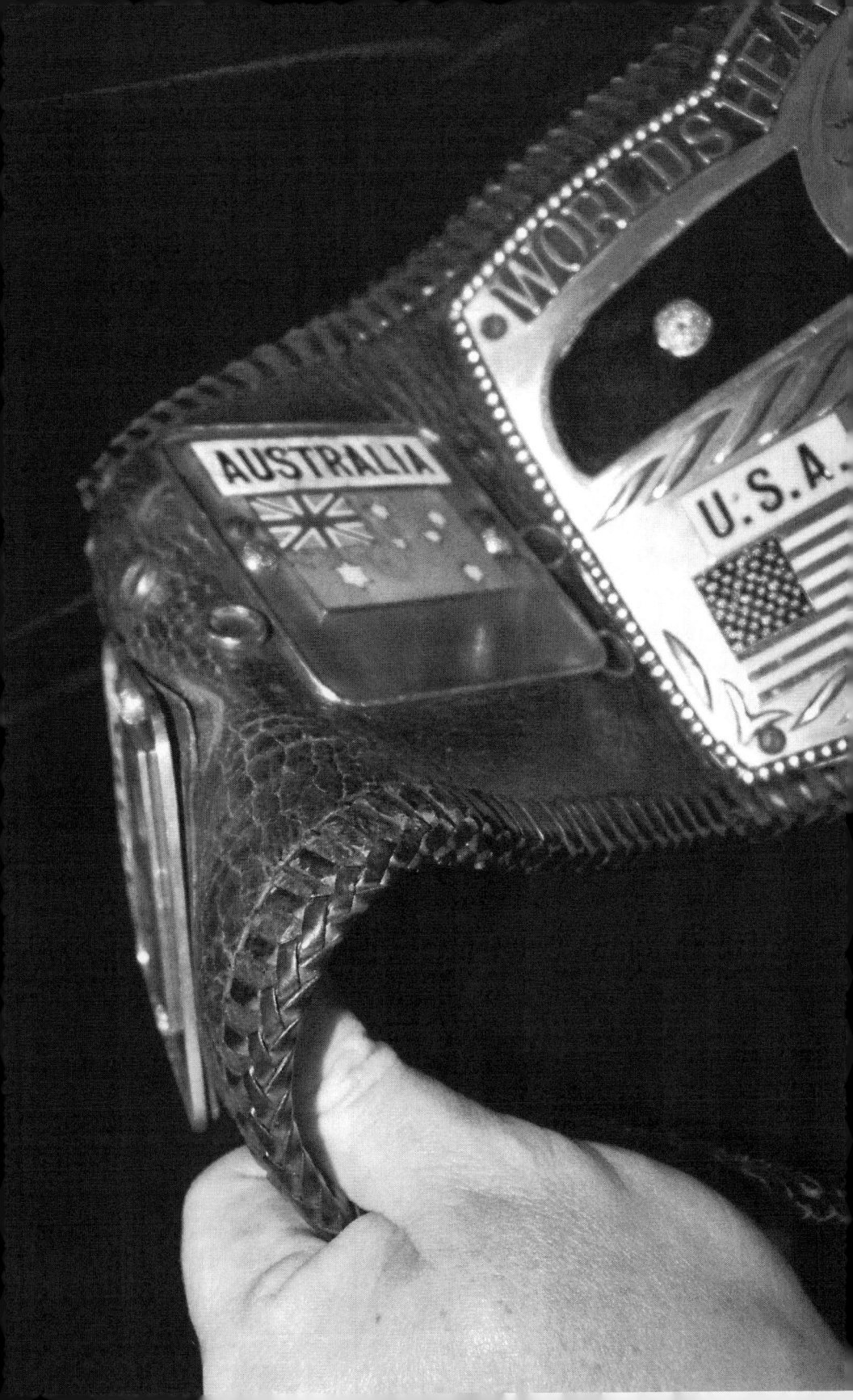

WORLD'S HEA

U.S.A.

Chapter Eight
All The Pieces Matter

A close inspection of the Ten Pounds of Gold reveals a great deal about how it was made. In these photographs, Dave Millican explores the belt and reveals some of the secrets of its construction.

In the photo on the facing page, if you look closely at the view of the side plate in the far left of the photo, you will observe the outer gold plate mounted on a thin metal plate. The two have become slightly separated over time. As mentioned earlier, gold is a relatively soft metal and the backing metal plate was required to keep the gold plates from bending and breaking.

You also will observe in this photo on the Australia flag plate the two sets of screws that attached the plate to the leather strap. These additional screws were likely inserted during the time the plates were removed and then reattached to new leather. They may have also been added for additional stability on the strap.

At the top of this photo you will see the large number of tiny screws used to attach various parts of the belts ornamentation to the base gold plate.

All of the pieces on the belt (the swirls, ornamental beads along the exterior, etc.) are attached with these tiny screws.

Also seen in this photograph are the grommets between plates, and the additional exterior screws used to securely reattach the plates to the strap in later years.

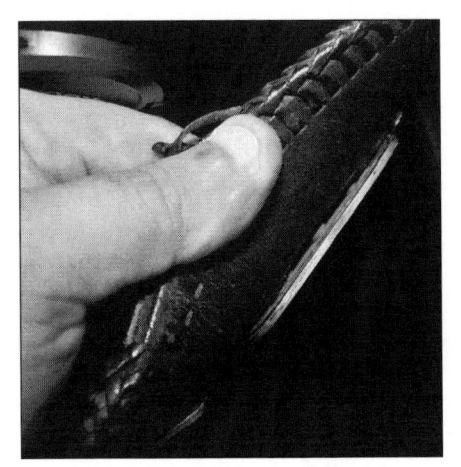

The photo above further illustrates the dual layers of plates, an outer gold layer affixed to an inner metal backing layer.

You also can observe the leather lacing around the edge of the leather strap coming apart after years of use.

On the facing page: a different view of some of the belt damage (missing hex-nut and outer beads). Plus an angled view of the cast wrestling figures and other pieces attached to the main plate of the belt.

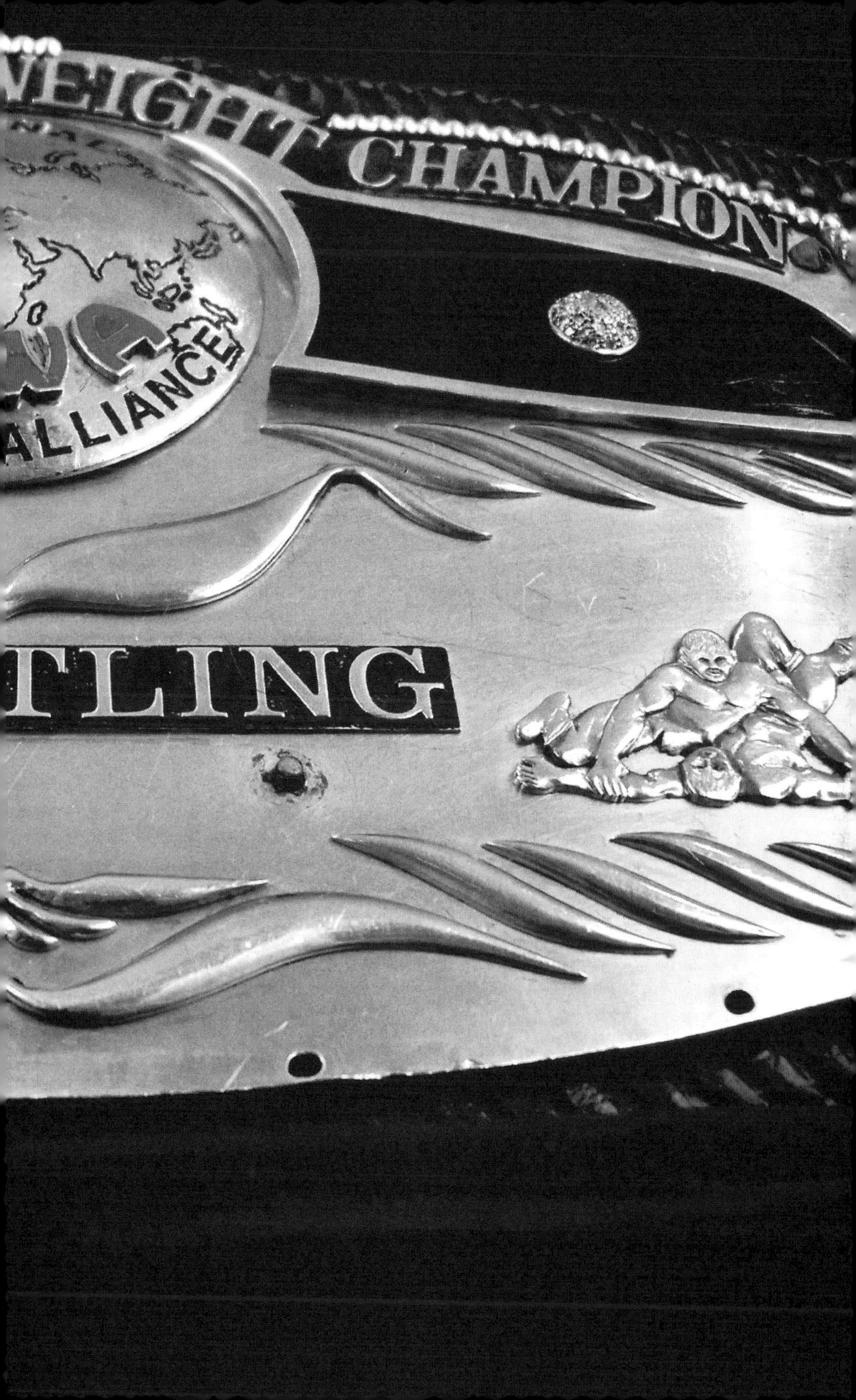
CHAMPION
ALLIANCE
TLING

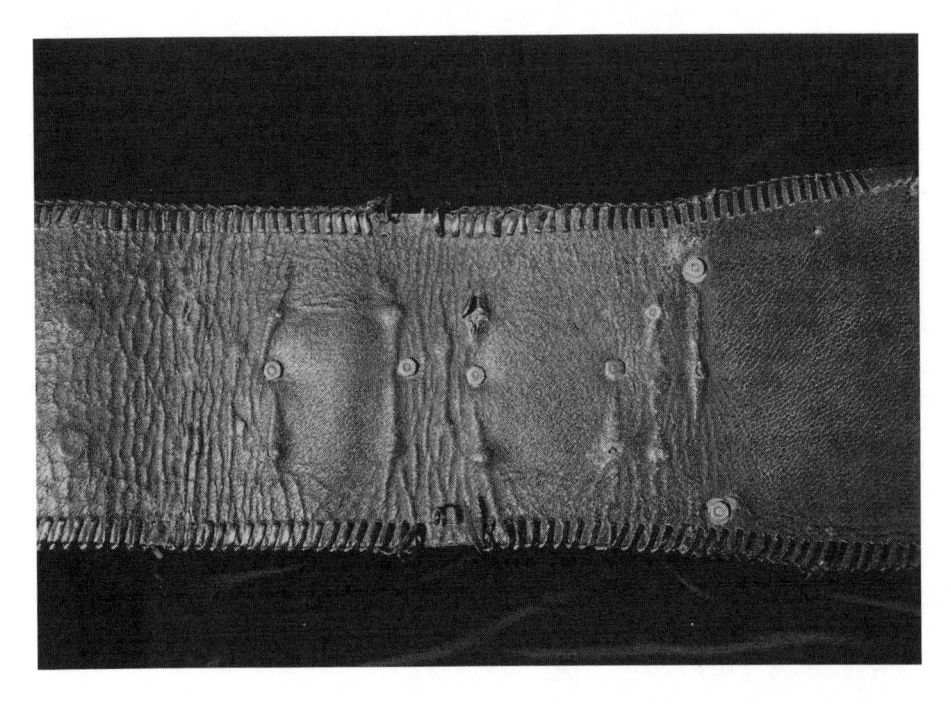

A close look at the back of the belt reveals the extent of the wear and tear it suffered over the years. The lacing is broken where the belt folds. You can see where additional screws were added to the main and side plates to secure them further over the life of the belt.

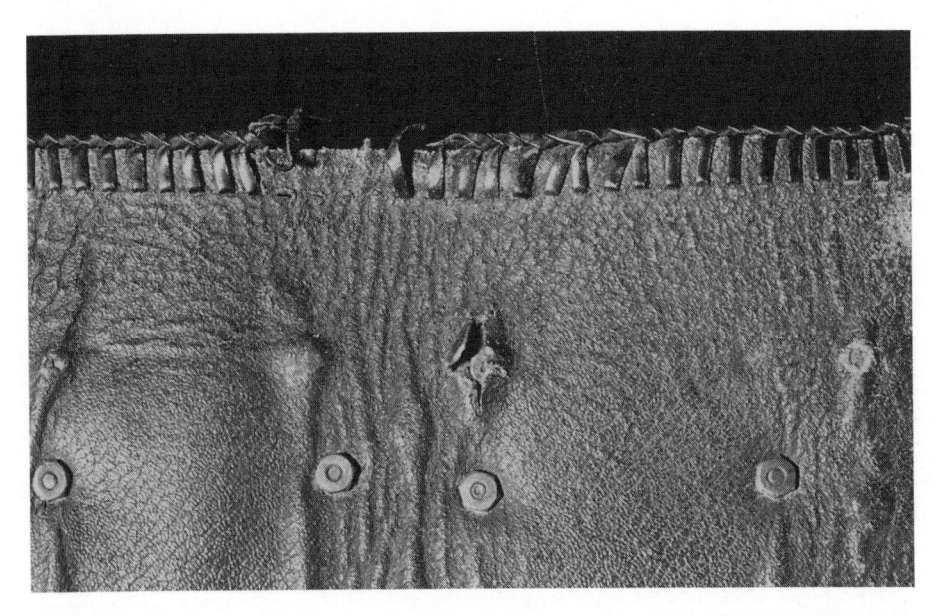

The Wrestlers

A closer look at the cast piece that depicts one wrestler pinning another on the main plate of the domed-globe belt.

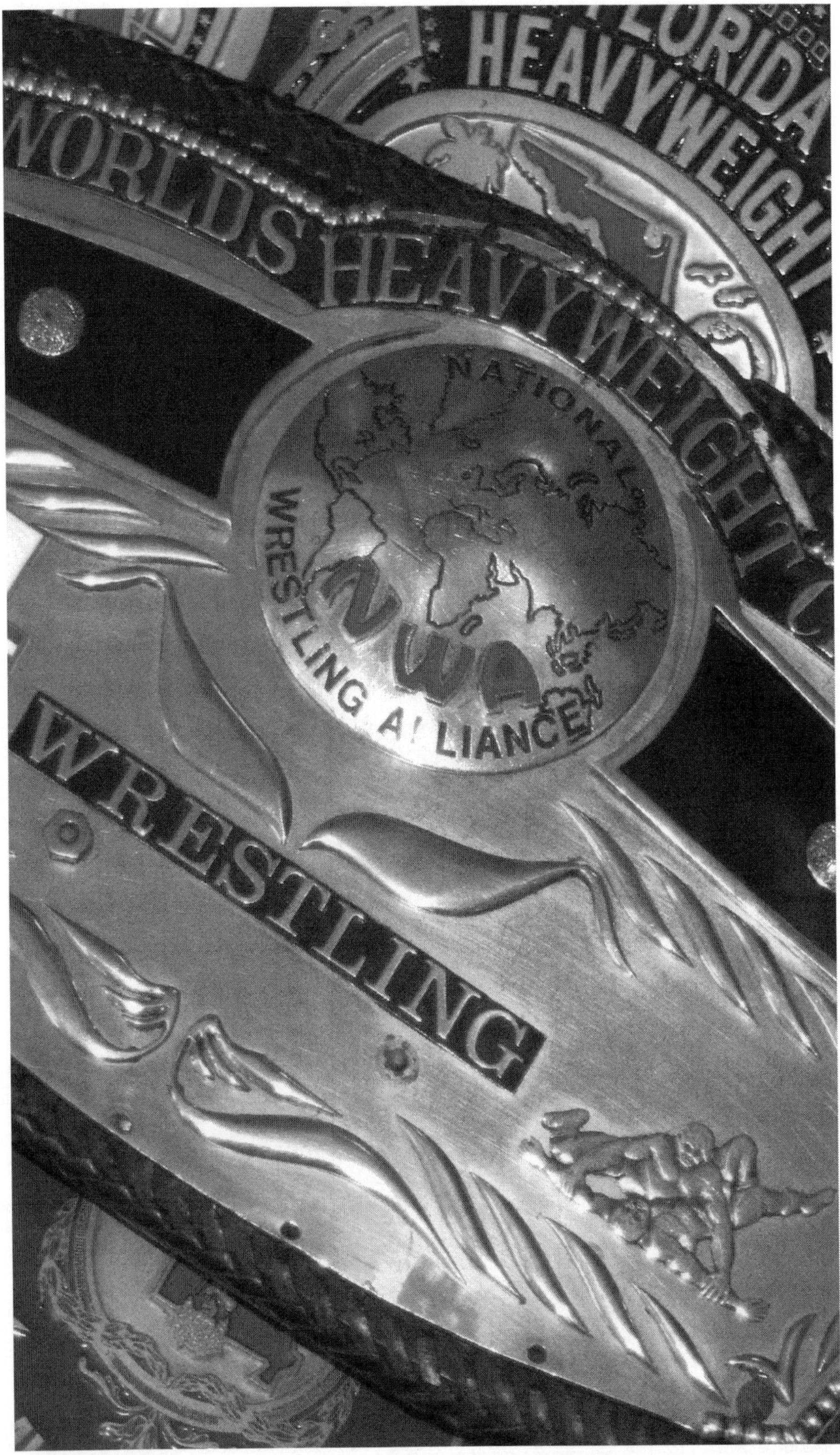
NATIONAL WRESTLING ALLIANCE
NWA
WRESTLING

Chapter Nine
Reunion

A special part of this project was the opportunity to reunite and photograph the NWA belt with other genuine artifacts from that same era. These included:

> (1) the United States heavyweight championship belt made by Reggie Parks and in service from 1983-1986,

> (2) one of Ric Flair's most famous robes from the 1970s and 1980s and worn most famously at Starrcade 83,

> (3) the iconic blue robe Kerry Von Erich wore in memory of his late brother David in Texas Stadium and throughout his short reign as NWA champion in 1984,

> (4) and the sterling silver and gold plated "Ric Flair" name plate that was attached to the "big gold belt" used by Jim Crockett Promotions as the NWA title belt beginning in 1986 and present on that belt through 1991.

The photographs on the next few pages represent the rare opportunity to see these great treasures together again, images that stir memories of the globe version of the NWA championship belt in its final few years of service.

It was the first time these treasures had been together in well over two decades, and likely the last time as well.

We also had fun placing the Ten Pounds of Gold beside replicas of some other famous NWA territory belts from that era.

TEN POUNDS OF GOLD

Ric Flair's Starrcade robe with the Ten Pounds of Gold on display at an event in Greensboro NC in 2008 celebrating the 25th Anniversary of Starrcade 83.

1983: Ric Flair is perhaps most identified with his grand collection of robes he wore throughout his career. One of his most famous robes was on display with the NWA belt at an event in Greensboro NC in 2008. In that same city 25 years earlier, Flair wore this robe into the ring as he prepared to challenge Harley Race for the NWA title. That night, Flair won the belt for the second time and was very emotional after the match (see photo on page 125) as he would later explain that so many within the business had counted him out, but he had come back and claimed it again. This time he did it in his own territory, in front of his Mid-Atlantic Wrestling fans. The robe became popularly known then as the "Starrcade robe", although Flair had been wearing it regularly since 1977.

1984: Kerry Von Erich defeated Ric Flair in Texas Stadium in 1984 to win the NWA world heavyweight championship in front of over 32,000 fans. The "Parade of Champions" show was promoted in memory of Kerry's late brother David. Kerry wore a beautiful blue robe into the ring that day which was emblazoned with the yellow rose of Texas. It was his personal tribute to his

Kerry Von Erich's Texas Stadium robe with the NWA belt.

brother. Kerry last wore this robe in Japan, the country where his brother had died, and where he would lose the title back to Flair. The image of the blue David Von Erich robe and the NWA world championship belt together are iconic for Texas Wrestling fans of the era.

1985: The version of the United States title belt seen below was in service from 1983 until early 1986 and worn by such great champions as Greg Valentine, Ricky Steamboat, Wahoo McDaniel, Tully Blanchard, Magnum T.A., and others. It was originally painted with red and blue behind the lettering on the belt, but by 1985 most of the paint had worn off, and Crockett Promotions removed what remained, which gave it the classic silver look it had when featured on national television beginning in 1985. The belt began to be known as "the Ten Pounds of Silver," an obvious reference to the common name used for the NWA world championship belt. The two belts were seen together weekly by huge national audiences in the mid-1980s on the cable superstation WTBS.

1986: Many fans may not remember that the original name plate for the Big Gold belt had Ric Flair's name misspelled "Rick" Flair when it first appeared in February 1986. It was an embarrassing mistake that was corrected a few months later when a new name plate was made by the silversmith with the correct spelling. During the interim period while a new name plate was being measured and hand made for the belt, Ric went back to wearing the Ten Pounds of Gold for a few weeks. He appeared on television with it at least twice, once in Birmingham, AL, on *Continental Championship Wrestling* and a second time nationally on WTBS on Jim Crockett Promotions' *World Championship Wrestling*. When the Big Gold belt returned around Flair's waist, it had a new name plate with the corrected spelling "Ric Flair."

When Flair left World Championship Wrestling in 1991, he took the Big Gold belt with him to the WWF, although it was later returned to WCW. In 1992, WCW booker Bill Watts put the belt back in service as the NWA world championship was reintroduced to wrestling fans and a tournament held to name the new champion. The title had been vacant since Flair left the company a year earlier. Watts removed the Ric Flair name plate from the belt.

Many may not remember until seeing the early photos in this book, but the Big Gold belt wasn't the only NWA world championship belt to have a name plate. The domed globe version of the belt originally had a name plate as well. For reasons still unknown, Jack Brisco was the only NWA champion to have his name on the Ten Pounds of Gold.

Across two generations: A rare and somewhat unusual photograph of the Ten Pounds of Gold alongside the Ric Flair name plate that graced the "Big Gold" belt, its successor.

Treasures new and old: At right, the genuine NWA world belt and U.S. belt with replicas of the Florida and Missouri state heavyweight championship belts, the latter two crafted by Dave Millican.

TEN POUNDS OF GOLD

Queen's Gallery
1212 THE PLAZA

Acknowledgements:
At The Gallery

It is difficult to find the appropriate words that adequately describe what it was like to spend an autumn afternoon with the Ten Pounds of Gold. It was very special for us to hold in our hands the very same NWA world heavyweight championship belt that had been held by some of the greatest wrestlers to have ever stepped through the ropes.

The belt is, as of this writing, in the possession of Ric Flair. For most of the past two and a half decades, it has been kept safely in a custom made case Ric had commissioned several years after the belt had been retired. It had been removed from the case only occasionally as Ric would bring it out for special television appearances, most recently in the weeks before his retirement match at Wrestlemania 24 in March of 2008. It's been back in the case ever since.

The belt was rumored to have been on display during Wrestlemania Weekend 2012 in Miami, fueling rumors that the WWE might now be in possession of the belt after some deal made with Flair. As of this writing, that can't be verified, but it actually would make us happy if that were to become the case. I know it might bother some old school fans to think Vince McMahon would own the NWA world title belt. But my thoughts are, who better at this point to make it available for wrestling fans of both past and future generations to see and enjoy? McMahon has done something similar with what old territory wrestling TV footage still exists that he owns, making it available on DVDs and his own

Queen's Gallery in the Plaza District of Charlotte NC.

on-demand cable channel. Most of this would have never seen the light of day otherwise. I would like to see The Ten Pounds of Gold held in highest regard, perhaps under glass and on display, for Dads and Moms to show their kids and tell them *that was the belt that the real world champions wore.*

When we went to Charlotte to photograph the belt back in 2008, Ric Flair would not allow the belt to be removed from the case unless overseen by Linda Ostrow, a friend of his for some 34 years who had designed and constructed the custom case at her art gallery and frame shop in Charlotte. Linda has known Ric since he first moved to Charlotte from Minneapolis in 1974; they shared the same beauty shop where the young rookie wrestler would have his hair dyed platinum blonde. Linda chuckled as she recalled the day back in 1974 that this huge wrestler plopped down at the hair dryer beside her one morning and introduced himself as the Nature Boy.

On October 28, 2008, I made the two-hour drive to Charlotte from Mount Airy as Dave flew in from Memphis. We brought

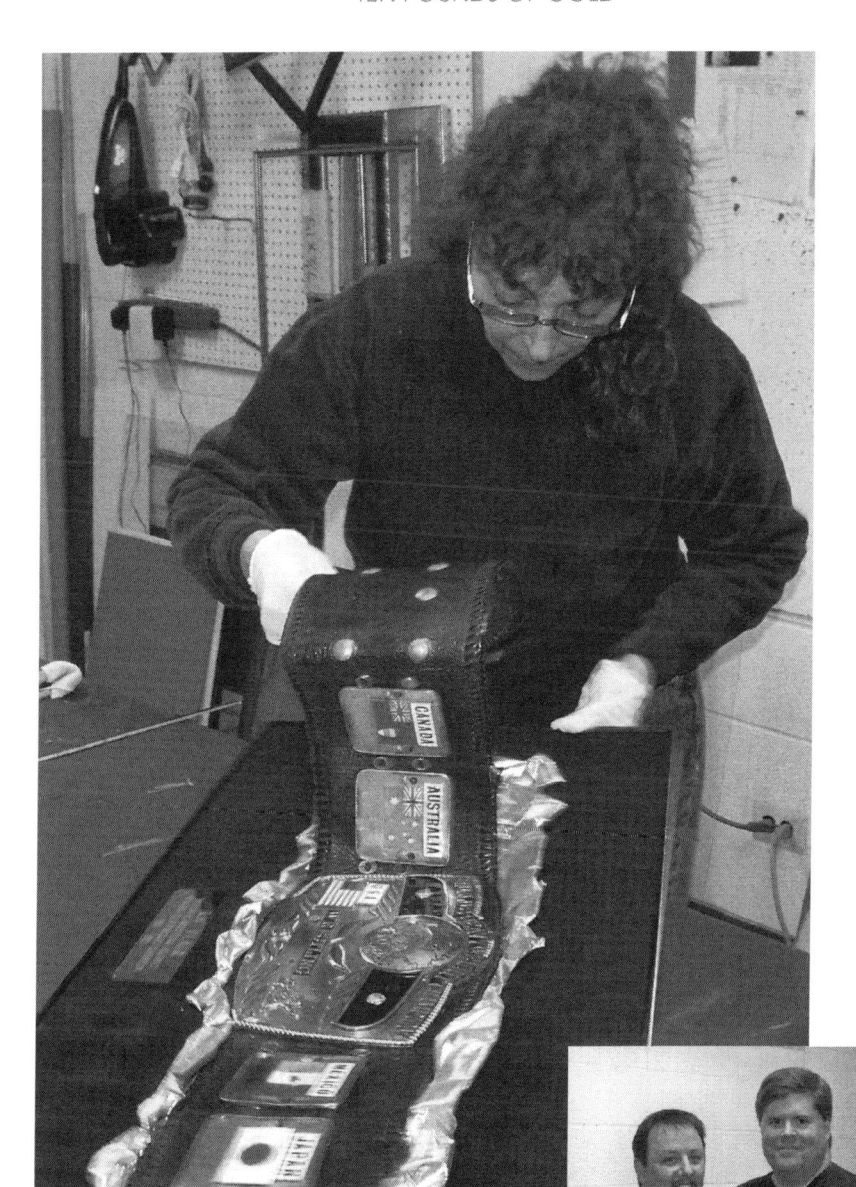

A the end of a special October day: Dave Millican and Dick Bourne (right) cradle the Ten Pounds of Gold before Linda Ostrow of Queen's Gallery in Charlotte, NC places the belt back into its permanent home.

The Ten Pounds of Gold is locked inside this custom case.
The plate below the belt reads:

"RIC FLAIR
NATIONAL WRESTLING ALLIANCE WORLD
HEAVYWEIGHT CHAMPION
1981-1991"

That beautiful belt sure does sparkle under those lights, just as it did under the lights of all those great arenas around the world where it was once defended.

the belt to Linda and she removed it from the case. We spent the better part of that afternoon taking the photographs you find in this book. It was one of the most exciting days two old belt marks could ever possibly have.

I want to thank everyone who helped make that day possible, especially Ric Flair for allowing us to photograph the NWA world championship belt; Michael Bochicchio at Highspots.com, whose enthusiasm and support for this project originally helped bring it to completion; and Linda Ostrow at Queen's Gallery.

Special thanks also to Harley and B. J. Race for their interest and support, and for their special contributions to this book when it was first published in 2009. Many of the additional photographs Harley provided are included in this Second Edition.

I also want to acknowledge the work that exists on this subject included in several books, including the autobiographies of Jack Brisco, Harley Race, and Terry Funk, as well as Tim Hornbaker's excellent book on the history of the National Wrestling Alliance. These were particularly helpful in research for the new material written for this Second Edition of the *Ten Pounds of Gold*. Thanks also to Libnan Ayoub for additional research on the belt's history, and to the photographers and rights holders who provided their work for use in the book; beautiful and memorable images of the great champions who wore the belt. All of these are credited in detail in the front of this book.

Thanks also to David Chappell, my partner in the Mid-Atlantic Gateway website. We will continue to document the history of our favorite little corner of the wrestling world and how the NWA world title played an important part in it.

I also want to say special thanks to my good friend Dave Millican for his encouragement and patience, and the ongoing education he has given me about the Ten Pounds of Gold.

- Dick Bourne

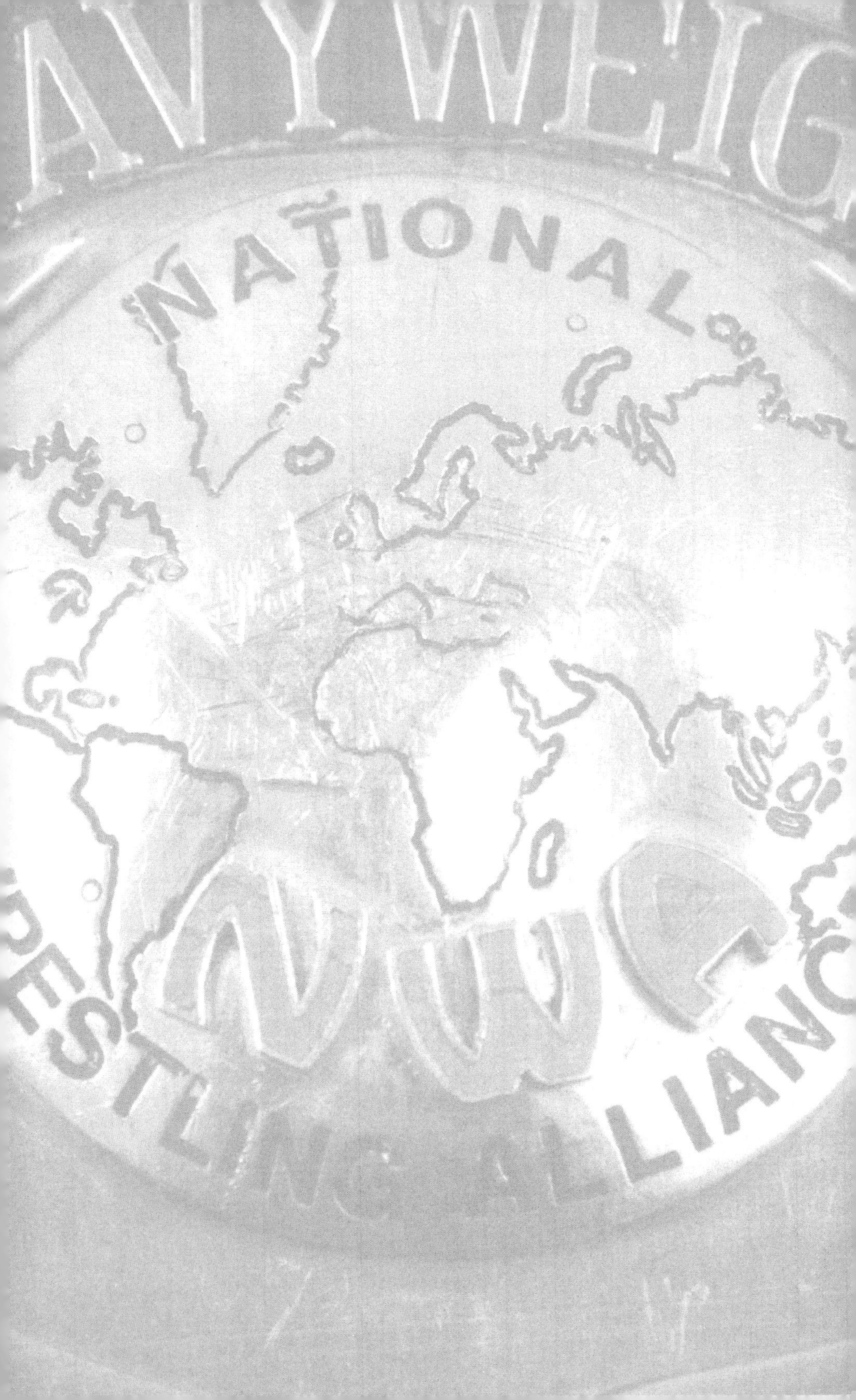
NATIONAL

Printed in Great Britain
by Amazon